Hitler Dances

Published now for the first time, *Hitler Dances* was first staged at the Traverse Theatre, Edinburgh, in 1972. Written in workshop rehearsals with the actors who performed it, the play explores individual attitudes to the popular myths of the Second World War. Hans, a dead German soldier, is theatrically resurrected and made to tell his story, into which are interwoven harrowing scenes from the life of a British woman spy sent behind enemy lines, captured and sent to her death.

Included is an introduction giving the background to the creation of the play.

D1489008

The photograph on the front cover shows a scene from the Traverse Theatre Club's 1972 production of Hitler Dances, *and is reproduced by courtesy of the Traverse Theatre Club. The photograph of Howard Brenton on the back cover is by Snoo Wilson.*

REVENGE
MAGNIFICENCE
PLAYS FOR THE POOR THEATRE
   (*The Saliva Milkshake, Christie in Love, Heads,*
   The Education of Skinny Spew, Gum and Goo)
BRASSNECK (*with David Hare*)
THE CHURCHILL PLAY
WEAPONS OF HAPPINESS
EPSOM DOWNS
SORE THROAT & SONNETS OF LOVE AND OPPOSITION
THE ROMANS IN BRITAIN
THIRTEENTH NIGHT & A SHORT SHARP SHOCK!
   (*A Short Sharp Shock! written with Tony Howard*)

translation

THE LIFE OF GALILEO *by Bertolt Brecht*

Howard Brenton

HITLER DANCES

METHUEN · LONDON

First published in Great Britain 1982 by Methuen London Ltd,
11 New Fetter Lane, London EC4P 4EE
Copyright © 1982 by Howard Brenton
Songs copyright © 1982 by David McNiven
ISBN 0 413 50060 8

Set in IBM 10pt Journal by 𝍇 Tek-Art, Croydon, Surrey
Printed in Great Britain by Richard Clay (The Chaucer Press) Ltd,
Bungay, Suffolk

In memory of Amaryllis Garnett

Introduction

Hitler Dances was first produced in January 1972 at the Traverse
Theatre Club in Edinburgh by the Traverse Workshop Company
under the direction of Max Stafford-Clark. The writing of the
play had taken five months, but its original inspiration came in
1970, when Brenton was visiting the Mickery Theatre in
Amsterdam with members of Portable Theatre, with whom he
was then working. In an interview with *Theatre Quarterly* some
years later, Brenton described the origins of the play:

> I saw children in Eindhoven, which was flattened twice
> during the war, first by the Germans and then by the
> Allies. It is now the world headquarters of the Philips
> Electrical Company. And at night in Eindhoven, the
> huge Philips sign, like a weird emblem, flashes every-
> where in the sky. I saw a bombsite there, with children
> playing on it, this heap of rubble — history. And the
> idea of a German soldier coming out of the ground
> became meaningful . . .

As with *Christie in Love* (1969), then, the starting point of *Hitler
Dances* was a single theatrical image, simple but enormously
powerful. It was this image that Brenton took with him when, on
the invitation of the Mickery Theatre (which also lent a certain
amount of financial assistance), he returned to Holland with
members of the Traverse company in October 1971 to begin
work on a play provisionally entitled *Hitler Dancing.*
    The final text of the play is a combination of a conventional
script and a letter from Brenton to the company written after
the initial rehearsal period, and it is this which provides the key
to an understanding of the sorts of methods and techniques that
were involved in its making. The text of *Hitler Dances* was not
presented to the Traverse company as a finished piece of work
that was purely of the writer's own making; rather Brenton's
initial idea acted as the basis for a collective exploration by the
whole company of the themes and possibilities it suggested. The
eventual form of the play owes almost as much to the work done
by the Traverse company members as it does to Brenton's formal
authorship. This was by no means a radical departure for Brenton
as a writer; his work with Brighton Combination and the students
of Bradford University in the late sixties indicates the importance
he attached to the productive sharing of ideas and experience

even quite early in his career, and it is significant that *Hitler Dances* shares many themes and techniques with those early plays, *Gum and Goo, Heads,* and *The Education of Skinny Spew* (all 1969). What was different in the case of *Hitler Dances*, however, was that with the Traverse company, Brenton was using a group that had been committed for some time to exploring and developing new relationships between writers and actors in the production of a play. Stafford-Clark, on becoming its director, had encouraged the Traverse Theatre Club to break away from its policy of producing 'straight' plays, setting up instead an independent workshop with a group of actors and musicians. The following comments, taken from an interview in *The Sunday Times Magazine*, March 1980, refer specifically to the work Stafford-Clark was later to do with the Joint Stock Theatre Company — when, incidentally, he again collaborated with Brenton on *Epsom Downs* (1977) — but they apply equally well to the methods used by the Traverse company in 1971:

> (The work) includes the actors, the director or directors, sometimes the designer, and of course the writer, and during that time there's no script. The ideas of the play are discussed, and improvisations are initiated, not necessarily by the director, and this period acts as a fertilising ground or greenhouse for the writer . . . The writer's free to incorporate any material or ideas that weren't discussed at all. The workshop simply acts as a way of being able to explore themes and ways of dramatising them . . . (Actors') creativity is rarely called upon. You gain their commitment if you say to them 'The script will finally be written by the author, but first we all have an opportunity to explore our own obsessions and create things from scratch, to explore, to initiate subjects.' You're tapping a source of energy that normally plays don't demand . . .

These were the circumstances of the making of *Hitler Dances.* The sense of the genesis of the play being as much a communal learning process as a piece of formal writing is vital to an understanding of its final form, though it is equally important to remember that, in the final analysis, the play is very much Brenton's own.

Nonetheless, the presence of the Traverse company is felt everywhere in the text. It is perhaps the least conventional of all

Brenton's plays. It is certainly the least accessible on a first reading. Its structure appears to be disjointed and fragmented: the two stories that are told constantly overlap and undercut each other, violently impacting together the people, places and historical situations that are separated in reality by many years and miles. Moreover, the play refuses to be pinned down into a single recognisable theatrical genre. Styles change with bewildering speed from gothic melodrama to breezy naturalism to two-dimensional satire; powerful images spring up, only to be savagely cut down by a sudden, deflating joke. The actor is required to 'snap' from comparatively straightforward naturalistic characterisation to the presentation of crude stereotypes and inanimate objects; from acting out the stories to telling them or commenting on them in song. Yet in many ways, *Hitler Dances* is also a simple play. With the exception of lighting, it makes few demands on the technical resources of the theatre. Only six actors and four musicians are needed; no set is specified; and only minimal costumes and hand-props are used. Brenton himself (in an unpublished interview with Philip Roberts and Malcolm Hay) describes the play's essential style as 'the sense of being fluid, working very rapidly, ensemble playing, the rapid creation and dismemberment of effects, the involvement of story-telling, the juxtaposition, stylistically, of things that are quite different in a very powerful series . . . ' The playwright's comments are those of a *practical* writer, concerned above all with the business of achieving his work on the stage, and it is this sense of the practical, of the intensely theatrical, rather than of the formal and the literary, that characterises the play. The script is suffused with the informality of a rehearsal: the actors' own names are used throughout, and the many stage directions are often personal in their tone and specificity. Indeed, the final shape of the play very much reflects the unusual circumstances of its making.

The workshops that Brenton initiated on arriving in Holland took as their starting point the image of children playing on the German soldier's grave, and were designed to explore and experiment with the group's own memories of the kinds of games they had played as children. Out of the careful re-creation of these games — and it should be stressed that the conditions of the work were in some senses more akin to those in a laboratory than to those in a conventional theatre — were formed the games the children play in the finished script, and although the scenes concerning the children are often not written as straightforward naturalistic pieces, they demonstrate the careful observation and recollection involved in showing how children really do behave. This personal research by the group also provided much of the material contained in the first narrative line of the play, the story of Linda and the dead German soldier, her 'dirty old man'. The company's work enabled Brenton to examine more closely the relationship between the child and the old man which he had already experimented with in *Gum and Goo* (1969), and contributed to its development as a dramatic metaphor for the relationship between the past and the present generally, a concern which characterises much of his work.

The company also used its childhood memories to re-create in detail the atmosphere of war-time Britain. Their recollections of rationing, of the sense of austerity, and of the 'togetherness' that existed during and just after the war, are incorporated directly into the text, particularly in the presentation of the wedding scene. More importantly, however, some of the personal memories began to suggest developments of the theme which was captured in Brenton's original idea, and which came to lie at the heart of the play. Each member of the group had in some way been personally affected by the war, losing relatives or friends. Their true stories are present in the play. In an article in *Theatre Quarterly* in 1972 (from which all subsequent comments by actors are taken), Carole Hayman describes her own experiences:

> I was born three months after (my father's) death. That's weird . . . We are left with this terrible residue of our families having been twisted and decimated by events which took place before we were born . . .

It is this sense of the pesent being pregnant with the legacy of the past that became the driving force behind the evolution of the play.

However, it became increasingly obvious that the indirect, 'second-hand' nature of the company's experiences — all were born towards the end of the war — was not in itself a sufficiently comprehensive approach to a subject as large and complex as that of *Hitler Dances*. The company therefore began to supplement its own memories with conventional historical research, and with interviews with members of the war generation, including Dutch resistance workers. Their findings not only began to undermine general assumptions about the nature of the war, but also

developed a sense of distance between the attitudes of the
company and those of the previous generation. This clash of
values is described by Kevin Costello:

> There's a total myth about the Second World War. My
> father was quite young when the war started. Yet he
> wanted to join up right away which is something
> inconceivable to me. I don't think you could ever have a
> mass call-up in England again. Too many people would
> refuse to fight. It's known that the only way those
> Battle of Britain pilots could get through their missions
> was to be pissed out of their minds all the time. That's
> what the characters in *Hitler Dances* say constantly —
> 'Back here in 1941 pissed out of our minds' . . .

Accordingly, the company undertook a more detailed examina-
tion of received attitudes regarding the war, and turned their
attention in particular to the treatment accorded to the subject
in films, both British and American. Again, the approach was
initiated by a group member, Sabin Epstein:

> Being born in the U.S. right at the end of the war meant
> I had to approach the subject very differently from most
> of the others. I was working in terms of the recall I had
> of the movies I had seen — rather than being able to talk
> to families who had actually lived through the Blitz or
> rationing and those kind of things. We did a lot of work
> originally on films — trying to recreate old war movie
> situations . . . British films concentrate on the fight for
> survival, defending a long cultural heritage . . .

Out of those improvisations came the second narrative strand of
the play, the story of Violette Szabo. The play's version is based
on the 1958 Rank film, *Carve Her Name With Pride*. The film
perpetuates the myths surrounding the war: it is a successful
commercial mixture of light comedy, romance, glib heroism and
glamourised violence. Research showed the inaccuracy of this
kind of presentation. Violette's mission was shown to be pointless
and doomed to failure before it began; her death was due simply
to administrative inefficiency. It was to this aspect of her story
that Brenton turned.

The experimental work done by the Traverse company provided much of the material for *Hitler Dances*; indeed, it supplied the 'meat' of the play in terms of locating the subject's central areas of interest. The early improvisations also forged what is the essential quality of the play: its profound and powerful sense of unease. Kevin Costello:

> Playing is an essentially positive act. But the children at play in *Hitler Dances* resurrect a dead German soldier . . . There's a going-back to the simple rituals — the ones a pre-literature theatre first grew out of . . .

It is this almost primaeval quality which induced that sense of 'nihilism and breakdown' — the savage cruelty of children, the obscenity of violence without a purpose — that Brenton was seeking. Yet the improvisations were not purely concerned with the exploration and definition of the intellectual content of the play. The playing of children's games is an established work-shop technique, designed to break down personal inhibitions, and to create the close-knit group identity and commitment that is vital to a collective project such as the making of *Hitler Dances*. The overall purpose of such work, as Stafford-Clark suggests, is to fire imagination and to stimulate the actor's personal creativity. This could take the form of building a stage character from elements of an actor's own personality. This was certainly the case with Kevin Costello:

> At first I wasn't aware of being anything like Potter. Then Howard presented me with a speech in which Potter lists a series of books, like *Paradise Lost* and Wordsworth's *The Prelude* which he claims will help the war effort. It was quite eerie because I'd read all the authors mentioned — and they are my favourite books! The speech was as much about a side of my character I often repress as about Captain Potter. Howard had spotted this during an improvisation and had used it to write that speech . . .

Perhaps more importantly, the specific talents and training of individuals could also be utilised. For example, Sabin Epstein taught a daily movement class to the rest of the group, and was encouraged to incorporate his own ideas into the playing of the dead German soldier rising from the grave:

> Originally Howard wanted a wholly horror situation. I
> suggested a combined image of Christ's resurrection and
> a Frankenstein monster. That helped greatly. When I'm
> really working I have to think through the whole
> business of rising from the dead. First comes my
> breathing, feeling air going through my fingers, wrists,
> elbows, shoulders — then eventually to the whole body.
> Then realising I am holding a gun — which immediately
> leads to other associations . . .

Epstein's comments stress the ways in which the making of *Hitler
Dances* tapped into the personal creativity of actors not only
intellectually but also technically; the company suggested both
many of the ideas present in the play *and* the appropriate
theatrical means of expressing those ideas on stage in front of an
audience. The enormous range and variety of styles which the
play contains springs directly from the individual and group
involvement of the actors throughout the process, and that
involvement also made possible the difficult task of sustaining
the kind of control and flexibility that the finished play requires.
The violent changes in pace and mood, the sudden switches in
location and time, and the need to portray not only different
characters but different *types* of characters, have all to be
conveyed almost entirely by the actor's use of voice, body
movement and use of the acting space. Brenton, in the Roberts
and Hay interview, describes the sort of preparation the actor
needs to meet demands such as these:

> (He) asks athletic questions. 'How are you going to try
> and pace yourself, how are you going to be confident
> enough to put one foot in front of the other, second
> by second, through this part?' And as athletes prepare,
> they prepare by strange processes — a high jumper
> might do circuit training. So they are like athletes . . .

This quality of 'athleticism' pervades *Hitler Dances*: it was
present during its making, and it must be present in its
performance if the precision and fluidity of interpretation that
binds the two stories together and gives the play its shape and
meaning is to be achieved.

Brenton has said that *Hitler Dances* is 'not a thought-out show,
it's a very emotional show'. Nonetheless, the development of the
two central narratives by the Traverse Workshop Company, and
their exploration of various theatrical means of presenting those

narratives on stage provided Brenton with definite ideas not only about the structure of this play, but about the structure of his writing generally. The search for a specific and precise theatrical form which can articulate the complex relationship between past and present dominates much of Brenton's work since 1972; one thinks especially of *Weapons of Happiness* (1976) and *The Romans in Britain* (1980). *Hitler Dances*, whilst in many ways representing an unusual and very different departure in the writer's career, nevertheless marks an important step in his development as a dramatist.

Richard Boon

Hitler Dances was written to be performed by the Traverse Theatre Workshop Company, and was first staged at the Traverse Theatre, Edinburgh, on 20 January 1972, with the following cast:

Sabin Epstein
Kevin Costello
Carole Hayman
Amaryllis Garnett
Linda Goddard
Tony Rohr

With music by 'Bread, Love and Dreams'

Angie Rew
David McNiven
John Ramsey

Lyrics by David McNiven
Directed by Max Stafford-Clark

One

KEVIN *as* HANS.

On the floor a German soldier's tin hat, filthy tattered great coat and rusted mud-clogged rifle.
The HANS *mask.*
AMARYLLIS *speaks aside.*

AMARYLLIS. Death of a German soldier, on the last day of the Second World War.

She puts the HANS *mask and uniform on* KEVIN.

The company cower back from him with kisses.

They give KEVIN *the voice for the mask with insults and catcalls.*
As long as this takes . . .

TONY. Eh! Hans!

LINDA. You, Hans, you.

TONY. Psst Hans old son.

CAROLE. Hans Hans.

SABIN. Hey you. Bosch.

AMARYLLIS. Hans! Hans!

SABIN. Bosch soldier!

Pause.

Nothing from KEVIN.

TONY. Eh! Hans.

LINDA. You Hans, you.

TONY. Psst Hans.

CAROLE. Hans Hans.

SABIN. Hey you. Bosch.

AMARYLLIS. Hans! Hans!

SABIN. Bosch soldier.

LINDA. German soldier boy.

TONY *makes a loud whistle, two fingers, over* SABIN's *shout of . . .*

ALL. Bosch!

Bosch!

Bosch!

Bosch!

Bosch!

Bosch!

Bosch!

Pause.

KEVIN *tries the first sound for the mask off their voices.*

They cut fiercely into that.

AMARYLLIS. Whatsa matter German soldier, wan' your mummy, big-big frau titty? Kiss kiss come to mummy.

CAROLE *turns her back on him.*

CAROLE. Kiss kiss kiss.

LINDA *turns her back, lifts her skirt on him.*

LINDA. Oy Bosch boy, whatsa matter, got worms in yer little Bosch sausage?

AMARYLLIS *pokes her tongue out at him, turns her back and lifts her skirt.*

KEVIN *tries the word 'sausage'.*

TONY. Fuckin' bloody kraut!

TONY *blows a raspberry, V-sign, flicks his crotch at him.* KEVIN *tries the word 'blood'. Tries hard, but trails off.*

Silence.

Then he takes one painful step forward. At that SABIN *at once aside, deadpan.*

SABIN. At the end of the Second World War, the German soldiers walked home.

A man in Holland told us of hundreds of thousands of German soldiers, starving like the people they had oppressed, walking on the roads back to Germany.

(*To* KEVIN:) Hans, you're so hungry you suck stones.

KEVIN. . . . Ck st . . . ones . . .

He mimes, slowly, picking up a stone and putting it in his mouth.

LINDA *walks by* KEVIN.

LINDA. You think of food, all the time.

KEVIN (*building it*): Black. Black. Black. Black. Black. Black — blood — sausage . . .

KEVIN, *both hands to his mouth, fingers exploring inside his cheeks.*

LINDA. Food food, Hans. Think of it all the time. Hot, black blood sausage.

KEVIN. Bla . . . Blo . . .

SABIN. Suck stones, Hans!

And KEVIN *hits the first word of his own making.*

KEVIN. S . . . Sau . . .

A . . . Sau . . .

Er .. . .

Sauer! Sauer! Sauer!

Sauer . . .

KEVIN, *repeat until the voice is independent, then as fiercely as you can into* HANS's *first speech . . .*

Sauerkraut! Black coffee! Beer!

Hot black blood sausage! Sauerkraut, steaming! Black coffee boiling! Beer all frothy!

CAROLE. When you last eat, Hans?

KEVIN, *wearily. Plods a few steps.*

HANS. Seventy-two hours, ninety-six hours.

He sighs.

Ago.

CAROLE. What, what you eat?

KEVIN. Meat.

CAROLE. What kind?

KEVIN. Human.

> Ja Human meat, on the bone. Big dead American. Boiled a bit of him.

> *He taps his helmet.*

> In my Vermacht tin hat.

CAROLE. Urr, what bit?

KEVIN. Big American bicep. Very fat. Had tattoo of naked lady, sitting on Empire State Building. Turned pink as it cooked.

> (*Wearily*:) Terrible days. Ja ja, terrible days.

AMARYLLIS. Keep walking Hans.

> KEVIN, *a step. Use a shambling mime of walking on the spot.*

TONY. Your shoes are pretty ropey Hans.

KEVIN. All . . . Frothy . . .

CAROLE (*sharply*): And your foot! You got bit by a dog!

> TONY *at once as a dog.*

TONY. Woof woof woof!

> *Runs out on all fours, bites* KEVIN *on the ankle, runs back to the group.* KEVIN *at once, shouting.*

KEVIN. Ten litres! Once I drank! Ten litres and still stood and sang!

> Freude, schoner Gotterfunken,
> Tochter as Elysium . . .

> *That half sung he near falls over.*

AMARYLLIS (*coldly*): Two hundred miles to home, Hans.

LINDA. You know you're not going to get there.

SABIN (*aside, deadpan*): What was the attitude of the Dutch, the French, the Yugoslavs, the Czechs, the Belgians, the Norwegians, to the German soldiers on the roads, in rags, limping back to the ruins of the Reich?

> *Pause.*

> Hatred.

> *Pause.*

The occasional killing.

Pause.

Silence.

All stare at KEVIN. *He turns to them, a half-gesture.
They stare back. He turns away and continues his trudge.*

*Music begins. Music 'effects', both amplifying and pulling
against the words.*

LINDA. What you thinking of now, Hans?

KEVIN. Thinking-of-now . . .

(*He speaks fast*:) . . . in the black blood sausage little lumps
of fat . . .

And boil up! Boil up! And the fat all sizzles in the black . . .

LINDA (*sternly*): No Hans.

KEVIN (*as he trudges*): No no no . . .

LINDA. No, what you think of *other* than food?

KEVIN (*wearily, automaton*): Thinking. Of. In.

In. In. In. In.

Suddenly vigorous, bright.

In the early days, Hitler Youth! I was a German boy with the
German boys. Bare to the waist, bashing tent pegs in the
dawn. At night, long blood sausages in big boilers. And the
Labour Corps, my worker's spade in a forest of workers'
spades, marching under the newsreel cameras.

*The other members of the company in turn impose
tiredness, cold etc on* KEVIN. *He continues his speech, but
taking each imposition into his performance.*

TONY. Hans, you're very tired.

KEVIN. And in the streets, honour.

Honour.

Putting the boot in, the honour.

LINDA. Hans, you're very cold.

KEVIN. Flags, banners and flags . . .

Our flag touched by the Führer's flag of honour torn and
covered with blood from the Munich days.

SABIN. Hans, the dog bite's got gangrene.

KEVIN (*fiercely*): Hobnail boots to the twisted face of the Jewish bourgeoisie! All was honourable! Horst Wessel we sang, growing strong and golden.

We were golden in the firelight, golden German boys. Eyes wet with tears, strong bare arms, warm to each other's side.

TONY. Hans, the poison's got your groin.

KEVIN. Millions!

Millions of us in the great show. Searchlights of Nuremburg carving the Cathedral of the Reich out of the black night.

Always night and marching to the dawn, torchlight on our golden faces, millions of us marching, toward where the sun rose in the PALACE OF THE GODS.

The music coming on strong.

They have to shout to KEVIN *over the music here.*

CAROLE. Hans, now you can't walk!

AMARYLLIS. Hans! You're done for!

TONY. Better crawl off somewhere Hans!

AMARYLLIS. Done for you're done for!

KEVIN goes down on one knee.

Music stops dead.

Silence.

AMARYLLIS (*quietly, with contempt*): Dying of a dog bite.

LINDA. You still got to tell your story though Hans, and you're glad you've got someone to tell it to.

At once KEVIN, *simply to the audience.*
Apologia.

KEVIN. You see, really I had a very good time when I was a kid. Sewed my uniform myself, wouldn't let my mother do it. And my badges, I was so proud I'd sleep with my badges on my pyjamas, and with a little torch look at them, under the sheets, when all the rest of the house was asleep. And in the long mirror, I'd stand in my uniforms. And in my fantasy, whisper shouts to the Führer.

A whisper.

Führer my Führer.

With passion.

Oh I was innocent in my youthful nazi boots, free in the German fields, kicking the fresh grass.

Music.

During the music KEVIN *takes off the greatcoat, helmet and mask, and lays them with the rifle in a cruciform, in the middle of the playing area.*

Two

KEVIN, *as himself, addresses the audience.*

At his feet, the HANS *regalia.*

KEVIN. Our German soldier. Rotted old corpse now, twenty-seven years on.

Say hello to all the nice people, Hans, you rotted old corpse.

KEVIN *lifts the greatcoat sleeve, as if it was a dummy, makes it wave to the audience. Lightly, Punch and Judy.*

Hello hello — Jawohl Zieg Heil.

KEVIN *stands, and speaks more formally.*

And our German soldier looks up, his dead man's eyes see burning bomber planes shining with the stars.

Forever.

And with him in his grave there's the whole rag-bag.

Second — World — War.

Mouldering away down there, stinking. Oooh the pong.

Blitzkrieg — Warsaw — shell shock — pattern bombing, Rotterdam Dresden Hamburg.

Ooh ooh, festering away.

Poor old Hans. Dead, in a scrap of ground some-where — any-where in Europe, with children playing on his grave.

Three

All as kids.

Lights all over, very bright.

AMARYLLIS. Let's all go out and *play!*

DAVID. Great nothing like a good *play,* get your knees good and dirty.

ANGIE. My ma'll go potty if I go out and *play* an' get dirty . . . But I'm gonna *play* anyway so . . .

She makes a rude sound poking her tongue out.

KEVIN. Playtime, great! Have a good yell!

He does an Indian yodel.

SABIN. Play!

He does an Indian yodel.

CAROLE. Play!

She does an Indian yodel.

LINDA. Yeh, but *what* we gonna play, tho'?

Pause.

AMARYLLIS. Um.

DAVID. Um.

ANGIE. Um.

KEVIN. Um.

LINDA. Um.

SABIN. Um.

CAROLE. Um.

TONY. Um.

Pause.

Um. Ah.

Pause.

Yeh!

Pause.

Well I tell you one thing. S' gotta be *war.*

LINDA. I don't wanna play war, I wanna play nurses.

TONY. Na. War's the only game. Nu'clear o' course. *Boom*!

LINDA. Nurses is a nice game. You can 'av a hospital, an' a pa-tient, an' visitin' hours . . . An children an' dads bringing grapes . . .

TONY. My brother says a nu'clear bomb explosion is so *bright* you all go blind.

He covers his eyes.

Like that.

He uncovers them.

Great eh? Blind like that.

He covers and uncovers his eyes, peekaboo.
He gets the others doing it, but not LINDA.

Blind . . . Like that!

Blind . . . Like that!

An' my brother says all the *metals* get *melted,* even your watch an' your glasses. An' your hair falls out, an' babies get born *freaks*.

Fantastic!

TONY, *as a deformed baby, pulling his hair*:

Mummmmmmmmmmmmmmmmmy.

Mummmmmmmmmmmmmmmmmy.

The others follow suit, but not LINDA.

ALL. Mummmmmmmmmmmmmmmmy.

Mummmmmmmmmmmmmmm . . .

LINDA (*very angry stamping her foot*). Stupid! *Stupid*! I think that's jus' *stupid.* War is *stupid*.

ALL *stop, looking at the two of them.*

TONY. Stupid?

LINDA. Stupid.

TONY. Yeh.

But war's not *soppy, wet an' shitty* like nurses.

LINDA. Yeh but with war you get *dead* an' that's *jus' stupid*.

TONY. Yeh but gettin' dead's what it's all about. In' it?

LINDA. Yeh but you get dead, an' what's the game in that?

TONY. Yeh but you don't *not* get dead in War.

LINDA. Yeh but you get dead an' you can't play. If you're dead, can't play at all! Can you so there.

LINDA *pokes her tongue out at* TONY.

TONY. Yeh but!

LINDA. Yeh but what?!

TONY. Yeh but!

TONY's *nonplussed*.

Yeh but . . . *I'm not playing no game that's soppy, wet an' shitty.*

TONY *pokes his tongue out at her, and gives a 'V'.*

AMARYLLIS (*shyly pipes up*). Know a game, I know a game!

TONY *and* LINDA *turn on her.*

LINDA. What?

TONY. What?

AMARYLLIS (*very shy*). Do, I do . . .

TONY. It War?

AMARYLLIS *nods.*

AMARYLLIS. Mmm.

TONY. Great!

LINDA *pulls a face.*

LINDA. Urrgh.

You get dead?

AMARYLLIS *shakes her head.*

AMARYLLIS. Nnnnnn.

LINDA. Great.

TONY *pulls a face.*

TONY. Urrgh.

AMARYLLIS *takes a deep breath.*

AMARYLLIS. But you get dead, very very dead, if you're not *sneaky.*

LINDA *and* TONY *look at each other and shrug.*

TONY. Be gettin' dark soon anyway. Whatsa name o' this new, soppy, wet an' shitty game then?

AMARYLLIS. Enemies.

TONY. Enemies? I know that game it's *great*! HNNNNNNNNNN!

TONY *machine-guns everyone.*
ALL *double up, play dead.*

AMARYLLIS. Ow!

ANGIE. Ow!

DAVID. Ow!

KEVIN. Ow!

LINDA. Ow!

SABIN. Ow!

CAROLE. Ow!

TONY *still standing.*

The others doubled up on the floor. A drum signal from JOHN, ALL *sit up. Doll-like.*

TONY (*aside*): Enemies is a kids' game, it goes like this.

ALL *stand.*

Two leaders.

AMARYLLIS *and* SABIN *jump aside.*

Pick armies.

AMARYLLIS *and* SABIN *pick sides.*

To AMARYLLIS: DAVID, KEVIN, CAROLE.
To SABIN: ANGIE, LINDA, TONY.

AMARYLLIS. Bags!

SABIN. Bags!

AMARYLLIS. Bags!

SABIN. Bags!

AMARYLLIS. Bags!

SABIN. Bags!

TONY. Each army goes to its country.

> *They do, one side singing 'God Save The King', the other side 'Zieg Heiling'.*

> *One voice starts the singing . . .*

Each country has four bricks.

> *Each army holds up their bricks.*
> *(Mime them — not important to actually have them. Tho' you could use apples instead.)*

The game is to capture the bricks. But if you're 'had', *like this . . .*

> *At once* CAROLE *and* SABIN *demonstrate. A smashing chase.*

> CAROLE *is caught.*

You're dead.

> CAROLE *raises her arms.*

But in the middle, in no man's land, you're safe. *Like this . . .*

> AMARYLLIS *rushes forward, straight at* KEVIN, *who starts, then rushes at her. She darts back into No Man's Land.* KEVIN *hits a blank wall, and can't touch her.*

> AMARYLLIS *makes a thumb and nose gesture at him.*

That's the game!

> ALL *shouting 'goody goody'. And the game begins.*
> *Play it for real, for sometime. Then suddenly drum from the band.*

> *Light change.*
> *Shadows and dark, and* ALL *in slow motion. A stylisation of the game.*

AMARYLLIS. My mum says her first dad, not my dad, but her first hus-band . . . died in the War. Of shrapnel.

> *Gently touches her stomach.*

There.

> *Spreads her arms.*

ANGIE. In our family, in the war. One of my mum's relations, got his head cut . . . sev-ered.

With a gentle gesture across the throat.

Right off.

Spreads her arms.

DAVID. My great uncle got it in the balls and my dad says . . .

Gentle gesture, holding his crotch.

My great uncle bled for three days, crawling, before he died.

DAVID *spreads his arms.*

TONY. Distant cousin of mine. Track of a German troop carrier, went over his spine.

Doubles over holding his back, then spreads his arms.

KEVIN. Yeh I got one of them, distant cousin died in the war. Burnt alive in a tank.

Spreads his arms.

LINDA. One o' my aunties was in an air-raid shelter. What got a direct hit. She wasn't touched. But the old woman next to her, sort of . . . burst with blood. In her face.

Gently touches her face.

And my aunty sort of died of fear.

Spreads her arms.

SABIN. My father, lost in the North African desert, saw a man eat his own hand.

Gesture, gently 'eating his own hand'.

And when the man eating his own hand had died, my father took the corpse and . . .

Gently mimes, entrails from stomach to mouth.
And at once over SABIN's *mime* CAROLE, *breezily.*

CAROLE. Me I was a blitz baby. Orphaned. Not that my mum and dad got bombed. No, it was terror. One bad night they gassed 'emselves.

Hands into ribs, mouth distended . . . And spreads her arms.

Song.
Sung by the company, without music.

Put his photograph away
Lay it face down in a drawer
Take it out on Remembrance Day
In loving memory of a war.

Down in the dungeons seven feet deep
Where old Hitler lies asleep
German boys they tickle his feet
Down in the dungeons seven feet deep.

Four

Drum.

Light change.
And they're playing the game again.
After a little while LINDA *stops playing. Stamps her foot.*

LINDA. Horrid, horrid, horrid game.

Stamps her foot.
Jumps away from where she stamped. LINDA *looks at a point on the floor a few feet away from where* SABIN *lies as the dead* HANS.

Look, a hole.

The others ignore that, an argument breaking out about who was had and who not.

Between whoever's not had at this point — written out for DAVID *and* ANGIE *here.*

ANGIE. Had you!

DAVID. Didn't!

ANGIE. Had you!

DAVID. Didn't!

LINDA. LOOK LOOK LOOK, HOLE! A HOLE!

They all stop and look.
A pause.
LINDA, *scared.*

There's a hole . . .

They back away, all but AMARYLLIS.

She approaches and looks down 'the hole.'

TONY. Maybe it's a rat.

KEVIN. Chuck a stone down.

DAVID. Watch it, they go for your neck.

KEVIN. Na rats is scared.

DAVID. If they're got in a corner, they go for your neck.

LINDA. My mum says, rats are the souls of murderers.

AMARYLLIS *stamps.*

At once, rat effect.

She shouts.

AMARYLLIS. ONE!

And points off fast, the rest of the company follow the path of the running rat, with their eyes.

AMARYLLIS *stamps.*

ALL. TWO!

AMARYLLIS *points where the rat runs.* ALL *follow it.*

AMARYLLIS *stamps.*

ALL. THREE!

The rat runs straight into the company.

ALL. AH!

And they jump aside.
This done for seven rats.

ALL. FOUR . . . FIVE . . . SIX . . . SEVEN . . .

And a pause.
All shocked.

DAVID. I got to go home for my tea.

Pause.

ALL *looking at 'the hole'.*
CAROLE *approaches, gingerly.*

CAROLE. 'Ere.

> *Points.*

> Down there.

> *Pause.*

KEVIN. What?

TONY. What?

CAROLE. Down there.

> AMARYLLIS, *eagerly.*

AMRYLLIS. 'Nother rat?

CAROLE. Hand.

> AMARYLLIS *stops dead.*

> ALL *dead still.*
> *Pause.*

TONY. Not the hand of *Dr Doom* stretching out to crush the world like a soggy lump o' plastacine.

CAROLE. Jus' a hand.

> TONY's *face falls, scared.*

> *Pause.*

DAVID. It getting dark, an . . . an . . . I really got to go home for my tea.

> SABIN *raises a hand.*
> *Claws it.*

> ALL *stare.*

> *A Pause.*

TONY. Yeh. I got to go home for my tea, too.

> *Pause.*

> *Drum.*
> *And light going down fast.*
> *At the drum, they all run off. Not* LINDA.
> *In a huddle to one side they shout for* LINDA *to follow them.*

ALL. Linda Linda, run.

> Linda, run.

> *She stands there staring.*
> *The light into the setting for the 'Resurrection Sequence'.*

Five

SABIN *does the 'Resurrection Sequence'.*

SABIN *works toward the corpse's recovery of breath.*

Light.

Music.

SABIN *on his way out of the earth . . . and a comedy routine for* CAROLE *and* KEVIN. *The voices of Mr and Mrs Everyday out of the dark. As if they were watching this resurrection on a telly screen.*
(NB. the soldier coming out of the ground's written here as a horror holy theatre piece. With CAROLE *and* KEVIN'*s dialogue, I want to destroy the image's holiness for a time by cheap laughs, but still hold its power. To lodge the corpse in the play as HARD as possible.)*

CAROLE. I don't think he's gonna manage it.

Pause.

KEVIN. I dunno. Jesus managed it. Have a choc.

CAROLE. Ta.

KEVIN. Didn't he.

CAROLE. What?

KEVIN. Resurrection. Jesus.

CAROLE. These chocs are plain.

KEVIN. No they're not they're milk.

CAROLE. Must be 'Good News'.

KEVIN. Yeh.

Pause.

What?

CAROLE. You know. There's a box full of plain, an' a box full of milk. An' a big bloke comes on an' does a karate chop, an' sticks the two bits together.

So you get plain an' milk in one box.

KEVIN. I asked for 'Black Magic'.

CAROLE. Didn't you look?

KEVIN. Jus' stuffed it in the bag didn't I!

CAROLE. Oh don't get shirty Kevin. Put the light on, an' look at the box, settle it once an' for all.

KEVIN. Don't wanna do that. Spoil the effect won't I.

CAROLE. Oooh.

KEVIN. What's the matter?

CAROLE. Poor thing.

KEVIN. Oh. Yeh. Well . . .

Pause.

Jesus managed it.

CAROLE. Yeh but Jesus was a corpse only for three days. But he's been down there for thirty years.

KEVIN. You 'ad the hazel nut?

CAROLE. No.

KEVIN. Funny.

CAROLE. I mean, in Jesus' case there was still something left *to* rise from the dead. Quite a lot, in fact.

KEVIN. I don't know. Tricky thing to do, even under the most favourable conditions. Ow!

CAROLE. What?

KEVIN. Marzipan in my filling.

CAROLE. Read that in the *Sunday Mirror* 'bout Jesus? 'Man From Outer Space'.

KEVIN. Oh yeh.

Pause.

Man from what?

CAROLE. Outer Space.

KEVIN. Oh yeh.

Pause.

CAROLE. Coming from outer space, he had superior medical knowledge.

KEVIN. Miracle drug in his loin cloth?

CAROLE. Something like that.

KEVIN. Kim Philby had micro dots on his contact lenses.

CAROLE. Well there you are. Imagine what a race of far greater intelligence than we, could achieve. Rising from the dead, be like taking the dog for a walk.

Pause.

KEVIN. Mate of mine, worked in a mortuary.

Pause.

Told me the body goes fast. *Very* fast.

Pause.

Juices in your belly melt the works.

Pause.

Yes! Within hours the old intestines are swishing about.

CAROLE. Ugh.

KEVIN. No good saying ugh. Its a process of nature.

Pause.

Break up of the intestinal wall within twenty-four hours after death.

Natural as a tree or budding rose.

CAROLE. I still say ugh.

KEVIN. My mate, my mortuary mate, says gases are also given off.

Pause.

Music growing.

One of the dead!

Pause.

Bang!

Music nearly over him . . .

They 'ad to hose the place down!

Music.

The passage ends with SABIN *standing, hands held up, one clutching the rifle, like a triumphant war memorial.*

Six

Bright light slammed on.

SABIN *standing there. Holds it a while.*
Then TONY *walks forward. They exchange the greatcoat, helmet,
mask and rifle.*

*This as informally as possible, so the pitch of the event's very low,
and* TONY *can start from flat bottom.*

TONY *as* HANS.
LINDA *as the Little Girl standing behind him.*

LINDA. Ey, mister . . .

TONY *starts. Tries to turn. Can't.*

TONY. Uh?

LINDA. You wanna watch it.

Pause.

TONY. Uh?

LINDA. Cops'll get you.

Like with dogs.

TONY. Uh?

LINDA. You know! Get dogs wi' nets, don't they. Dogcatchers.

Well *cops* get old men wi' nets. *Dirty* old men.

(*Skittishly*:) You a dirty old man?

TONY. Uh?

LINDA. Dirty old men catchers, come an' get you!

She chants that.

Then straightforwardly . . .

You'll get washed all over. Cops do that when they catch
dirty old men, wash 'em all over.

I hate being washed all over. My Mum calls me a dirty little
slut.

TONY. Uh?

LINDA *comes nearer, sniffs and holds her nose.*

LINDA. Poo! Don't you stink! My mum says *I* stink, but I don't stink as much as you.

How you get to stink so much?

TONY *attempts to say something, but fails.*

TONY. Uh.

He sags, depressed.

LINDA. Want a go with my yo-yo?

She yo-yo's the yo-yo.

You have a go.

Hands him the yo-yo. He drops it.

What's the matter with you? Haven't you ever seen a yo-yo before?

She picks it up, puts it in his hand.

He stares at it.

She takes it away.

You've got to wind it up.

She winds it up.

I'm not going to keep winding it up for you. There look! Whee . . . !

She yo-yo's a few times. Then gives it to him.

He stares at it.

Look you put it on your finger.

She puts it on his finger.

Go on! Whee it!

He does, clumsily. Then building it up.

HANS. Wh . . . Wh . . .
Wh . . . Wh . . .

Wwwwwwwwwwwhe!

Whee!
Whee!

He falls over.
The yo-yo flies off his finger.
He sags, depressed. Looks up.

They eye the yo-yo.

Then he reaches forward snatches the yo-yo. And gives it back to her, gently.

LINDA. Want a sweet?

He takes the sweet. Looks at it.

Then with a gesture towards himself ('Old world courtesy') . . .

TONY. Hans.

Points at her.

LINDA. Linda.

Pause.

Go on you eat it.

He moves the sweet toward his mouth.

Blackout.

Seven

The lights slammed up.

AMARYLLIS *and* CAROLE *there, as bitchy little girls.*

HANS *slinks off fast,* LINDA *shoving him.*

She turns to face the girls.

CAROLE. There's that Linda Goddard.

(*Calls out:*) Linda Goddard, what you got in the woods?

CAROLE *and* AMARYLLIS *snigger.*

LINDA *stock still.*

(*They say 'snigger snigger' — get a rhythm in it.*)

CAROLE.
AMARYLLIS. Snigger snigger snigger.

(*They chant:*) If you go down in the woods today . . .

Snigger snigger snigger.

LINDA *turns on them and give them a 'V'.*

LINDA. Bugger off.

CAROLE. Oooh!

AMARYLLIS. Oooh!

CAROLE. She said Bugger.

AMARYLLIS. Linda Goddard, said Bugger!

They circle her.

Big word for a little weedy girl. Very big DIRTY word . . .

CAROLE. Where you get that big dirty word, Linda.

AMARYLLIS. Little goody goody Linda Goddard . . .

CAROLE *cutting across* AMARYLLIS *here.*

CAROLE. Little goody goody Linda Goddard, with a big dirty word like that . . .

AMARYLLIS. Got it from her dirty old man . . .

CAROLE. Get that big dirty word, from your dirty old man? . . .

AMARYLLIS. Course she did. Cos her dirty old man saw Linda Goddard's knickers.

AMARYLLIS *and* CAROLE *push* LINDA *tentatively.*

CAROLE.
AMARYLLIS.   Snigger, snigger, snigger snigger.

Faster.

AMARYLLIS. 'E saw her knickers!

CAROLE. Dirty old man see your knickers!

AMARYLLIS: Linda Goddard showed her knickers to a dirty old man!

CAROLE. Show us your knickers.

AMARYLLIS. Show us your knickers Linda.

They punch LINDA.

*On the floor she whirls round viciously, and speaks . . .
coldly, oddly, frightening the other two little girls.*

LINDA. Bugger you.

Pause.

Bugger you.

Pause.

Bugger you.

CAROLE *and* AMARYLLIS *back away, frightened.*
Then they look at each other, smugly and turn away.
Lights go down.

Eight

And up again at once.

AMARYLLIS *and* CAROLE *as* MOTHER, SABIN *and* KEVIN
as FATHER.

Up on each other's shoulders — they loom up over LINDA.

AMARYLLIS. Like — a — dirty — little — slut — oh — dear.

Handkerchief.

LINDA. Don't, Mummy.

AMARYLLIS. Covered in mess.

LINDA. Don't, mummy.

AMARYLLIS. Sopping in filth.

LINDA. Don't, mummy.

FATHER *looms up.*

SABIN. Linda!

LINDA *turns to 'him'.*

LINDA. Don't, Daddy.

FATHER *strides through the scene.*

SABIN. Linda, Mrs Hayman's little Carole, just along the road, says you've been taking sweeties from a funny old man.

AMARYLLIS. Going out of my mind. Sniff. Tug at my handkerchief.

SABIN. And your mother's going out of her mind.

AMARYLLIS. Harry do something.

SABIN. Yes. Eh. Well. Where's my pipe?

AMARYLLIS. Linda, Daddy wants to tell you something.

SABIN. Yes. Eh. Well.

Pause.

Linda! Have you been smoking my pipe?

AMARYLLIS. Go — on — tell — her!

SABIN. One must be subtle about these things. Now. Yes-eh-well. Linda. Your mother and I have been watching you grow up.

Pause.

I am watching you grow up.

Pause.

Into the world. Annnnnd you're a pretty little thing.

I mean girl.

Pause.

God help us all.

LINDA (*chirps up, at once*): Daddy I think your pipe's on top of the television.

SABIN. *Oh good girl!*

FATHER *strides away . . .*

Ah here it is! *Good heavens woman the bowl's all clogged up. Where are my pipe cleaners!*

AMARYLLIS. In your sports jacket dear.

FATHER *goes 'off'.*

Now Linda. What your father was trying to say was.

Pause.

That.

Pause.

That . . . There are men in the world.

Pause.

Who are wrong in the head.

Who do things.

LINDA. What things?

AMARYLLIS. Nasty things.

LINDA. What kind of nasty things, men in the world who are wrong in the head, do?

AMARYLLIS. Nasty, twisted, horrid things.

LINDA. Do do! But what they do!

AMARYLLIS. Things like . . . Take you away into the woods.

LINDA. But I like the woods.

AMARYLLIS. Oh dear, sniff sniff, my little girl.

FATHER *back on fast.*

SABIN. Not the waterworks again. And I can't find my pipe cleaners *anywhere.*

AMARYLLIS. Harry, speak to her.

SABIN. At a time like this my pipe gets clogged in the bowl.

AMARYLLIS. Harry, tell the *Little madam the little slut.*

SABIN. Um. Ah.

Linda! Come here.

LINDA. Going to tell me 'bout what the men do in the woods Daddy?

SABIN. Going to tell you about . . . The World.

Yes, The World.

Now Linda, remember that apple you ate for tea?

LINDA. Ugh, it was wormy.

SABIN. Well Linda, that's what the world is like. Wormy.

Yes. Now we're getting somewhere.

LINDA, *keen on the idea at once.*

LINDA. You mean that UNDER the world there's BIG WORMS crawling about, an' BIG MAGGOTS, all under the ground, an' sometimes the BIG WORMS an' BIG MAGGOTS poke their heads out right thro' Australia?

FATHER *appalled.*

A pause.

SABIN. Not . . . Quite . . . Linda.

LINDA (*sad*). No. S'pose not.

I mean, you'd see 'em sticking up more wouldn't you, I mean
if there was *giant worms* down there, you'd be walking along
the road, an' they'd *pop up*.

Pop!

The MOTHER *and* FATHER *jump, startled.*

Thro' the road.

They stare at her.

High as a house, cos they'd have to be *really giant* worms.

SABIN. Linda . . .

LINDA. High as Big Ben.

SABIN. Linda!

LINDA. 'Ave mouths big as the bulldozer knocking down our
school.

SABIN. Linda! *Shut up.*

At once LINDA *turns on the tears.*

SABIN. Dying for a smoke . . .

AMARYLLIS. Tug tug tug . . .

SABIN. Some obscene . . .

AMARYLLIS. Tug tug . . .

SABIN. Get his hands on our . . .

Light going down. LINDA *keeping her wail up, the Mother and
Father figures going backwards, out of the light.*

AMARYLLIS.　　　Tug, tug, tug, tug . . .
SABIN.　　　　　Worry worry, mouths all furry

Nine

Lights down for a second, then up dimly around LINDA.

'In LINDA's *room'.*

LINDA. Up in my room. Night time. List'ning for *Boogjees*

Boogjees is animals. That I know's there. They got spines, on
their fingers with *webs* between, an' eyes all *goggly* an'

scarey, an' *mouths of blood.*

An' I like them, an' *Boogjees* like me. An' they make a cat noise.

Out of the dark from the other members of the company, the BOOGJEE *noise.*

And when I hear the noise, I know the *Boogjees* are going to take me away.

And take my old man away, the Boogjees will take me an' my old man away to *A Happy Land.*

CAROLE. And, dead of night, Little Linda, tiptoes down the stair.

SABIN. In the dark, out the back door.

TONY. Snakes, all the bad creepies . . .

LINDA. Mice with *sharks teeth* an' . . .

AMARYLLIS. Steals her daddy's torch . . .

LINDA. Pussy cats who bite ladies tits *an' all kinds* of nasties . . .

The lights faded out to blackout.

(*In the blackout a torch must be got to* LINDA.)

. . . But my Boogjees are not nasty, and they look after me.

CAROLE. And the little girl walks through the dark, out of the town, over the field, with her kindly monsters at her side.

And into the wood.

(*Song.*)
Out in the dark night
damp and wet
the boogjees wander by
all night long
in the wind and storm
you can hear their mournful cry

Feather and fin
Skin and scale
A terrible shout
and a horrible wail
The Boogjees shuffle
head to tail
By the light in their eerie eye

Down where the dark swamps
suck and sigh
the Boogjees walk alone
where the moon
grows pale too soon
you can hear them
sing their song

> With dread intent
> The Evening's spent
> In weaving webs
> Of discontent
> and tying knots
> in peoples' thoughts
> Til you think that you were wrong

When you're lying awake
in the dark or your room
and your eyes are struggling
to pierce the gloom
when your thoughts are disturbed
and your mind runs wide
that's when the Boogjees
step inside
They chew at your thoughts
and gnaw at your brain
until you imagine
you're quite insane
but come the light
of a dismal dawn
the Boogjees fade
and at once are gone
You're left to know
and feel no more
except for a dread
you can't ignore
for they have left
their mark behind
on the innermost workings
of your mind
Now as the sky breaks
white and wide
they have no more to say
where the seaweed marks

the ebbing tide
you can watch them
pass away

> Finger and nail
> Horn and claw
> A fearful face
> and a padded paw
> scratch and scritch
> til your nerves are raw
> And you long for the break of day

Ten

In the dark.

LINDA (*whispers*): Hans!

Pause.

Hans!

An owl's toowitawoo.

LINDA *excited.*

I run away. And I come to live with you. An' we'll go all over the World. An' never mind your bad leg, an' your bad arm, an' never mind your bad all of you, I'll look after you. Like the little girl in the picture, and the old man selling balloons on the road . . .

Silence.

The torch, she switches it on in her own face.

Hans.

LINDA *sweeps the torch beam round, and catches* TONY *as* HANS, *moving, scared along a wall.*

TONY. Huh huh . . .

He tired to back out of the torch beam.

LINDA *flips the beam onto her own face.*

LINDA. Don't be scared Hans. S'Linda.

Flips and beam onto TONY

TONY. Linda?

LINDA goes over to him, holding the torch on his face.

He puts a hand out.

TONY. Got − me − a − knife?

LINDA. Got you food. Cornflakes. An' we can milk cows in the fields for milk as we go along.

HANS *getting excited.*

Great difficulty.

TONY. *Got me a knife?*

LINDA. Got my mum's kitchen knife here you are.

No sight of the knife.

HANS *hurriedly hiding something in his clothes.*

What you want a knife for?

TONY. A . . . Ammm . . .

LINDA. A What?

TONY. American G.Is.

LINDA. What's G.Is? Some kinda *creepies*?

TONY. American G.Is − everywhere.

LINDA *cheerfully.*

LINDA. Don't you worry, my *Boogjees* got claws and'll keep G.Is away.

Slight pause.

She touches his hand.

Ooh in't you cold. Lemme give you a cuddle.

The torch out.

Blackout.

A pause.

KEVIN. But early next morning.

Lights up at once.

LINDA. Ooh its cold. Horrible cold.

TONY *staggers to his feet, pulling* LINDA.

TONY. Linda. We go.

He waves ahead. LINDA *yawns.*

LINDA. Somewhere nice? We go somewhere nice?

TONY (*waving vaguely ahead*). Berlin.

LINDA. Where's that?

TONY (*waving vaguely ahead*). Berlin.

LINDA. It far?

TONY *waves ahead and falls over.*

He tries to drag himself forward with one hand pointing ahead with the other.

Oh you silly old man, you gone an' fallen over, again.

TONY..Chan — cellory — Garden . . .

LINDA. I'll sit you up, just one more time.

Little girl with a great big doll . . .
She sits him up.

TONY *reaches forward again . . .*

TONY. Brandenburg Gate.

LINDA. Don't be silly you silly old man.

TONY *hangs his head.*

LINDA *stamps.*

Silly old man.

Glares at him.

Silly!

She sticks her tongue out at him. No reaction.

She stamps and whirls away.

I'm going home.

At once TONY *tries to stop her, tries to catch her hand, topples.*

TONY. Huh huh huh . . .

She turns stamps puts her tongue out and is going away again.

A great effort from TONY.

Tell — you — story.

Pause. LINDA *turns.*

LINDA (*sharply*): Story 'bout what?

TONY. Don't – go – Linda.

LINDA. If I don't go you gotta tell me story, story 'about
what?

HANS. Story 'bout war.

LINDA. How stupid.

She flounces away.

TONY, *after her.*

TONY. Story about . . . *girl.*

LINDA. Was she pretty?

TONY. Very pretty.

Pretty – as – you.

LINDA *huffs at that.*

LINDA. An' was she clever?

TONY. Very – clever.

LINDA. And did she grow up?

TONY. Beautiful – young – woman.

*TONY draws his hands down in the air, the figure of a
woman.*

Not like the joke, dead serious, putting the grown VIOLETTE
there.

And before them, a spot comes up, gently, on AMARYLLIS.

LINDA. Her name pretty too?

TONY. Very – pretty.

Pause.

Violette.

LINDA. That IS pretty.

Pause.

Violette.

Eleven

Gong.

All the company in a waltz.
They spill away into the dark.
Light brighter on AMARYLLIS *and* TONY. *As an*
announcement.

AMARYLLIS. The dead German soldier tells the little girl the story of Violette.

TONY. The daughter of a French woman and an English working man, Violette was a lively child.

LINDA. Whee!

LINDA *cartwheels round the stage − tin whistles from the band.*

TONY. Grew to a woman, twenty-one.

LINDA, *as the Little Girl, out of breath.*

LINDA. And did . . . And did Violette . . . Get married?

TONY. She − Got − Married.

Spreads his arms over the scene.

First − And − Last − Romance.

The band begins a gentle, romantic waltz.

On the 14th of July, 1941, Bastille Day, her mother told Violette to go out and find a brave French officer, so lonely in Wartime London.

And bring him home for tea.

AMARYLLIS *walks around looking at several of the company, then glancing down embarrassed.*

SABIN. Ow beautiful iz ze English park. But ow eavy iz my 'eart. Stranger in a strange coun-try.

TONY. French Legionaire! Brave Heroic Soldier! Nature holds her breath!

LINDA. Oooh Hans what happened then, 'E fall in True Love . . .

TONY. Wait − for − it!

SABIN *and* AMARYLLIS *look at each other.*

A cymbal crashes.

TONY. Love at first sight!

True love and all nature agrees!

AMARYLLIS. Bonjour monsieur.

SABIN. Bonjour, mademoiselle.

ETIENNE *a little salute and a bow.*

VIOLETTE *looks down modestly.*

A pause.

SABIN. Le ciel est bleu, aujourdhui.

AMARYLLIS. Oui monsieur, le ciel est très bleu aujourdhui.

SABIN. Aussi les arbres sont très jolis.

ANGIE *and* CAROLE *as two girls watching a film.*

ANGIE. What they saying?

CAROLE. She says good afternoon Monsieur, 'E says good afternoon mademoiselle. 'E says the sky is blue today, *she* says yes the sky is *very* blue today. To which *'E* replies, also the trees are very pretty.

ANGIE. Ooh in't that lovely.

KEVIN. 'Ere, what you make of this load?

DAVID. Love story in't it.

KEVIN. Yeh.

He sniffs loudly.

But what you make of it?

DAVID. Load o' juice.

AMARYLLIS. Monsieur, please come back to my house.

ETIENNE *shocked.*

SABIN. Mademoiselle, I am shocked, I . . .

CAROLE. OH!

ANGIE. What what!

CAROLE. She's asked 'im back!

ANGIE. OH!

AMARYLLIS, *blushing.*

AMARYLLIS. Oh no monsieur . . . It is the 14th of July. My mother said, bring a French officer to eat with us . . .

SABIN. Mademoiselle, you are beautiful and kind.

SABIN bows, takes AMARYLLIS' *hand and kisses it.*

CAROLE. First touch!

ANGIE. I saw I saw!

TONY. They had a whirl — whirl — *whirlwind romance.*

With a one . . .

He breaks down, falls over.

With a one — a one . . .

A ONE TWO THREE . . .

The band begins the waltz again.

The company dance.

SABIN *with* AMARYLLIS, KEVIN *with* CAROLE, TONY *shambling with* LINDA.

SABIN. Will you marry me, Violette.

AMARYLLIS. Yes I will marry you, Etienne.

Into a wedding march with the recipe for a wedding cake.

TONY. Bake a cake in war-time England.

CAROLE. Powdered eggs with love.

KEVIN. Quarter pound dried raisins.

LINDA. Stain the cake with siver of oils.

TONY. To make it look fruity.

CAROLE. Margarine in the marzipan.

KEVIN. And two months coupons for the sugar.

LINDA. Sugar to go in the icing.

AMARYLIS *and* SABIN *as bride and bridegroom come through the arch.*

There's a flash. Wedding photograph.

Waltz stops.

From JOHN *the funeral bom-bom on the drum.*

SABIN *embraces* AMARYLLIS *and turns away.*

Two little waves.
These gestures are automaton. Brief.

Then the announcement from KEVIN . . .

Twelve

Music for this passage

Chords that drag out blow by blow on the top of JOHN's *funeral drum.*

TONY (*aside*): Death of Violette's husband, Etienne, in the North African Desert, at the Battle of El Alemain.

AMARYLLIS *in the centre. At the back* KEVIN *as* INSTRUCTOR. *In the foreground* SABIN *as* ETIENNE *in the desert, lit by a spot that starts white and another that bleeds in red as the passage goes on . . .*

KEVIN *gives the blow by blow actions of* ETIENNE's *death. The company goes through them by rote.* SABIN *repeats them, as 'the* ETIENNE *actor'.*

KEVIN. You're running. Bullet hits you. Left thigh.

Forces your leg forward.

Drum.

Twist your body with it.

Drum.

Fall to your right. Right knee.

Drum.

Involuntary contraction. Left calf twists. First scream.

Drum.

Silent scream from SABIN.

Second bullet hits you, left-hand kidney.

Drum.

Bullet exits through intestines, you clutch the hole.

Drum.

Immediate rush of vomit to your throat.

Drum.

From the small of the back, paroxysm.

Drum.

Curves you, pull pull. Tight-as-a-bow.

Drum.

SABIN *back over on the floor.*

Two fearful wounds but still conscious.

Drum.

You crawl. For two hours.

Drum.

You go blind.

Drum.

Hallucinate. On a sand ridge, the cross of Jesus.

Drum.

You crawl near, reach out.

Drum.

Nailed on the cross, cruciform the melted metal gut of a desert tank.

Drum.

A pause.

Nightfall.

Drum.

Your wounds as deep as the World.

Drum.

Drum.

Act of contrition.

SABIN, *very fast.*

SABIN. Oh my God I am sorry and beg pardon for all my sins

and detest them above all things, because they have crucified
my Lord Jesus Christ and most of all because they have
offended thy infinite goodness and firmly resolve by the
help of thy grace never to offend thee again and carefully
to avoid occasions of sin for ever and ever. Amen.

Drum.

Drum.

KEVIN. And you're dead.

Light change.

AMARYLLIS *comes forward. With grief and gaiety.*

AMARYLLIS. Dreary.

'Due process.'

Knock on the door, and telegram.

'Father forgive me for I have sinned — In what manner
daughter — ugly thoughts of hate father, against the dirty
German swine who killed my Etienne — wash these thoughts
from your soul my daughter with the blood of Jesus Christ
who died for us — *I'll wash with blood Father, all the
fucking krauts.*

She laughs, at once out of that . . .

Traditional scene! How Violette got widowed. There was
a knock on the door, and my mum went. It was a telegram.

Her mother looked like stone. Mum, looked like her face
was stone.

And its funny, cos the telegram felt heavy. And reading,
Violette thought — its his tombstone, and the absurd phrase
'Memorial Plaque' popped into my head.

I couldn't stop thinking — 'Memorial Plaque'. Plaque. Clack
clack.

Clack clack.

Said 'Regret to inform. In Action. Due process of burial.'

Clack clack.

Dreary, all the world went dreary. Clack clack it went. How
you get widowed, with a clack.

Widow weeds, widow weeds, how I was a widow weeds. Old

bag on the Common, in black, on the Common benches old bags in black. No teeth.

She laughs.

When I was little I thought that was what a widow was. Old bag with no teeth, sitting on a bench on Clapham Common. Please teacher what's a widow?

She's hysterical . . .

Don't you know what a widow is? Old — woman — with — no — teeth . . .

She pulls her lips over her teeth . . .

Ummmmmmmmmmmmmmmmmm.

She comes out of that, and at once . . .

Violette is only twenty-three.

She pauses. Then, gaily . . .

My mum comes from a mining area in France. Artois. Women have a black shawl on the back of the door. When the sirens of the mines go whoop whoop, meaning there's a tragedy, they put on the black shawls. And run to the pit head gates.

For they may already be widowed. And to go bareheaded, and married, would be tempting fate. Asking . . .

She falters.

God's wrath.

She pauses.

Cut out.

Like having a brutal man with a meat knife. Burst into the room. One cosy afternoon when you're having tea. And hit you, hack at you, and cut out a lump. All . . . bleeding.

And rush out the house, never saying a word, and leaving you, all cut out. Bleeding.

A pause.

They wouldn't tell me how he . . .

She can't say died, searches for a euphemism.

spent his last . . . times.

Only, if he died in North Africa, he must have . . .

died . . .

in the sand. And it must have been . . .

hot.

And I know he crawled. Somehow I know he crawled.

At once she's cheerful.

And I picked myself up! And I dusted myself off. And I became a killer. A.T.S. Ack Ack. Battery outside Newcastle. Planes come to bomb the Tyneside. And with my little gun bang — bang — bang!

Fancy officer, took me out. Said it wasn't lady-like, lady-like to like it so, frying jerry in the sky. Heinkels like Sardine Cans chucked into the fire, inside nasty jerry fish sizzle sizzle.

Change, fiercely.

And in my heart I know he went blind too, crawling in the sand. I know he went blind.

Savagely.

Burn! And Germany will be a desert. And all the Germans will crawl in the desert, that once was their Hitler Reich. And these were the thoughts of Violette, and she became a heroine.

Blackout.

End first half of the show.

Thirteen

After the interval, light on the playing area.

A glimpse of the company coming on, the lights going down.

Blackout.

Silence.

In the dark, AMARYLLIS *and* CAROLE.

AMARYLLIS. Atrocity?

We gonna see some A — tro — cit — y?

A pause.

I get bored a lot.

A long pause.

Like a bad cold. Boredom.

A very long pause.

Don't you Carole?

CAROLE. What.

AMARYLLIS. Get bored.

CAROLE. I dunno.

A long pause.

Not much.

AMARYLLIS. I dunno.

A pause.

I may, o' course, any moment now get raped.

CAROLE. Yeh.

AMARYLLIS. Some maniac, may leap out.

Pause.

Blond, wild blue eyes, with a razor.

CAROLE. Make a change.

AMARYLLIS. Yes.

CAROLE. Article in the *News Of The World* last Sunday, 'bout suicide.

AMARYLLIS. Well, s'nice for them who has what it takes.

CAROLE. I dunno. Don't take much. Razor blade.

AMARYLLIS. Yes. But you got to have what it takes.

CAROLE. I s'pose so.

Pause.

AMARYLLIS. Went to the flics last night.

CAROLE. Oh yes.

AMARYLLIS. Bloke disembowelled 'imself.

CAROLE. What in the cinema?

AMARYLLIS. No, on the screen silly.

CAROLE. Wonderful what they can do.

AMARYLLIS. Saw 'The Devils' the week before, an' all. That geezer, with 'em smashing 'is legs.

A bright spot slams on.

CAROLE *into it.*

AMARYLLIS, *fiercely.*

AMARYLLIS. War story. Violette. Simple, healthy girl, played on Clapham Common.

And now she hates the German Nation.

CAROLE *viciously.*

CAROLE. I wanna kill a German!

Change.

She shrugs. And gaily:

I just wanna kill one that's all. Do my bit. Like all the millions of boys out there. Do my bit, for . . . (*A slight mispronunciation:*) Civ − lisation.

Blackout.

A pause.

'I'm sorry that I made you cry.'

AMARYLLIS. What?

CAROLE. What?

AMARYLLIS. What you said then.

CAROLE. Oh, that song.

Pause.

AMARYLLIS. You only saw his legs in a flash. They only showed them to you, in a flash.

Pause.

All splintered.

CAROLE. Saw a photo the other day, of a man who'd been through a wind screen.

AMARYLLIS. What he look like?

CAROLE. Funny.

AMARYLLIS. Funny?

CAROLE. Not 'funny ha-ha.' Just funny.

AMARYLIS. Oh.

CAROLE. Man in 'Softly Softly' the other night, vomited.
Been a fuss about it.

AMARYLLIS. It's when they get it in the stomach I can't stand.
It.

CAROLE. That is nasty.
Brain that gets me. When they get it in the brain, it gets me.
Have a Treet.

AMARYLLIS. A What?

CAROLE. Chocolate coated peanuts, you know. THE . . .
Chocolate coated peanut.

AMARYLLIS. Thank you very much.

CAROLE. Know them seances. Summoning up the dead.

AMARYLLIS. Oh yes.

CAROLE. Voices coming through. And all that.

AMARYLLIS. Oh yes.

CAROLE. Well, listen.

Fourteen

In the dark.

And someone or thing stumbling around.

KEVIN *as* POTTER

KEVIN. Oh damn and blast!

A match flares — KEVIN's POTTER mask briefly.

Turns his fingers. The match goes out.

Damn.

Pause.

Got a funny feeling there's an upturned bottle of scotch

in here, running away. Dripping through the floorboards. Like life.

Match flares again. He's on his knees.

There's an empty bottle of scotch before him on the floor.

He approaches it by the light of his match.

The mask looks up.

Captain Potter here! Back here in 1942. Pissed out of my mind too. God I rymed must be far gone.

Ow!

The match burns his fingers.

He flicks it out.

Sound of him scrabbling with the box.

Another match flares.

A lot of people were, back here. Pissed out of their minds in World War Two. Messerschmidt Pilots were on Methadrene. Buzz English Airfields convined they were birds, eagles falling on prey. But their cannon were empty. Hnnnnnnnnnn. Empty.

And they all died. Ow.

Match out again.

LINDA *at once in the dark.*

LINDA. Captain Potter, drinking in a little room . . .

KEVIN. Chink!

LINDA. . . . In the Ministry of Pensions Building in Whitehall.

KEVIN. Now I can't find my bloody glass!

CAROLE (*at once, as* VIOLETTE): Knock knock!

KEVIN. Damn!

CAROLE. Can I come in?

KEVIN. Bloody light.

CAROLE. This letter said come here.

KEVIN. Who are you?

CAROLE. Don't you know? You wrote me a letter.

KEVIN. Look, eh, come in.

CAROLE. I am already in. What a funny smell.

KEVIN. It's a rather seedy little room . . .

CAROLE. What you got the blackout up for? It's a lovely day outside. Get the blackout down an' open the window.

KEVIN. There is no window.

CAROLE. Coo, you have it rough in the Ministry of Pensions.

KEVIN *strikes a light. They look at each other.*

This is the Ministry of Pensions?

Pause, the match flickering between them.

CAROLE, *fast.*

You wrote me a letter, my contributions were not in order and you had a query, please be here at two-thirty . . .

Suddenly a big bulb overhead goes on.

KEVIN *momentarily lets the match burn on. Then he shakes it out.*

CAROLE. You're pissed.

And you're not the Ministry of Pensions, are you?

A pause.

KEVIN. Let's . . . Go and walk in the park.

Light change. He offers CAROLE *his arm.*

LINDA (*aside*): St James's Park. Winter. Cold, but sunny.

KEVIN *arm in arm with* CAROLE.

He stops.

They break apart.

KEVIN. I was 'the intellectual at war.'

An Idealist. Locke, Berkeley, Hume, would roll the Panzar Divisions back into the Rhine. Kierkegaard, Aquinas, Kant bomb the German Chancellory.

Oh how superior the conduct in war, of a man who knew Wordsworth's Prelude by heart. Compared to the buffers,

the stupid pig-eyed army buffers, farting in the Army and
Navy Club staining the leather armchairs.

I prided myself! In the beginning, I really did pride myself.

That because I read Paradise Lost, what's more read
Paradise Lost for pleasure.

I would win the war — humanely.

A pause.

But as the war went on, it became very clear to me. That I
was just one more nasty young man, drinking his own piss and
calling it wine.

I drink my own piss and call it wine.

JOHN *on the xylaphone begins 'Oranges and Lemons.'*

CAROLE. What's your job?

KEVIN. I select people.

CAROLE. White slaver are you?

CAROLE's VIOLETTE *here, talkative, playful. Skipping
round him.*

Combing the woman's services for talent?

My mum told me where to kick white slavers. With my
regulation toe cap of my regulation flat heel. And my big
brother says that if you hit anyone there, on the lip . . .

She touches POTTER's *upper lip.*

There, they end up crying. Un-controlably. Makes the nerves
go all haywire.

She pretends to hit him.

He flinches.

An' my YOUNGER brother taught me this!

She flies at him, puts a powerlock on.

Power lock!

JOHN, *'Oranges and Lemons' building up here . . .*

KEVIN. My leg!

CAROLE. That's the point, its ON the leg!

KEVIN. You're a very strong girl.

CAROLE. We're an athletic family. My mum can lift the dining-room table with one hand.

KEVIN. Eh, people are looking at us.

CAROLE. Oh yeh.

She laughs. They untangle. Stand. She asks for his arm, with a bow he gives it her.

Suddenly music stops dead.

KEVIN. He died at El Alemain.

(*Nastily*): Your husband.

CAROLE *frozen.*

Pause.

In the sand.

Pause.,

Now you are on an ack-ack unit. Just outside Newcastle. Shoot German planes down. In your minds eye, you see the Germans inside the German planes, burning alive.

'Oranges and Lemons.'

Sung very loudly, full band. Dead stop.

CAROLE *quietly.*

CAROLE. Want me to go to France don't you.

KEVIN *quickly.*

KEVIN. You will train in Scotland. You will be given the rank of Second Lieutenant in the Woman's Catering Service. You will secretly train for a parachute badge.

CAROLE. Whee Kerflop!

She cartwheels.

KEVIN *stares ahead ignoring her.*

What's the matter mate, still pissed?

KEVIN *shakes his head and looks down depressed.*

Cheer up you just recruited me. I'll be one of your star turns! End up a bloody heroine!

KEVIN. Yes. Won't you.

End up a bloody heroine.

Music.

And a dance of 'Oranges and Lemons.'

VIOLETTE *cartwheeling.*

Fifteen

Lights up on TONY *as* BRIGADIER BADGE.

Uniform front. Cap. Mask with moustache. Game rifle.

TONY. I know I am a parody of myself.

He hiccups.

Pardon.

BUT back here in 1942, there is a war on.

Hiccups.

Pardon. Bit pissed. BUT.

AMARYLLIS (*announcement aside*): On a grousemoor, somewhere in Scotland, Brigadier Badge who is not a happy man, is killing little birds.

TONY. Bang!

He shoots. An actor flutters to the ground. Another as a dog pads to the 'bird'. Brings the bird back to BADGE's *feet, in its mouth.*

The dog wags his tail.

DOG. Woof woof!

TONY. I know I am a parody of myself. Bang!

Another bird flutters down, the DOG *brings it to* BADGE's *feet.*

DOG. Woof woof!

TONY. But back here in 1942, there *is* a war on.

Therefore, though I may be repulsive as a person . . .

The rest of the company make sick noises.

ALL. Ugh ugh ugh . . .

BADGE, *over that.*

TONY. And tho' my . . .

He stutters.

The 'ughs' die away.

D . . . D . . . Dental trouble may bring forth uncalled for ribaldry in the officers mess.

ALL (*as twit officers*): I say, the Brigadier's got B.O. in the mouth, ha ha ha.

TONY. There is a war on!

(*Stutters:*) D . . . D . . . D. . . I have high hopes of it!

He adopts a huntsman's pose. Foot on the dead couple of birds before him.

That personal defects, little personal defects m . . . m . . . may go to the wall!

And a new era be ushered in. And true fellowship will begin, and barbarism depart.

LINDA (*aside*): Says the poor old fool quoting Winston Churchill.

TONY. And at the end of the tunnel there will be a new

G . . . G . . . G . . .

KEVIN (*aside*): And the poor old fool goes into a paroxysm and then . . .

A pause.

Roars out.

TONY. GOLDEN AGE!

And at once TONY *up with his gun.*

TONY. BANG BANG BANG BANG!

. . . and all the remaining members of the company flutter down as birds. The DOG *goes mad with 'woof woofs'.*

DOG. Woof woof woof woof woof woof . . .

And the DOG *as fast as he can gets all the corpses at* BADGE's *feet, and comes to heel. Panting.*

TONY. You see, back here in 1940 . . .

KEVIN. He clenches his fist, with panic.

TONY *clenches his fist with panic.*

TONY. You've got to have faith. Got to have a BURNING DESIRE TO save Civilisation.

A burning . . .

KEVIN. The poor, ugly, brutal man has great difficulty to find the right words, for his heart — is — so — heavy . . .

TONY *violently, difficulty in breathing, think of him actually having a heart disease . . .*

TONY. Determination . . .

Burning determination, burning realisation . . .

That the Hun is at the door, that . . .

THE COMPANY. And the poor, brutal man seizes up.

Silence. TONY *as* BADGE *in tableau, foot on the dead animals, gun in hand.*

TONY. Violette.

A pause.

Lovely . . .

He hiccups.

Girl.

Was instrumental. Yes, can say I was . . .

Suppresses a hiccup.

Instrumental.

Quickly.

Sorry pissed out of my mind but back here in 1942 . . .

Hiccups.

Violette. Trained her.

Blackout.

Sixteen

SABIN *and* KEVIN *come forward and announce.*

Music hall style.

SABIN. Ladies and gentlemen . . .

KEVIN. At enormous cost . . .

SABIN. For you . . .

KEVIN. Here . . .

SABIN. Tonight . . .

KEVIN. Mr Tony Rohr . . .

SABIN. Will now do his . . .

KEVIN. Brutal English Officer . . .

SABIN. Brutal training routine . . .

KEVIN. Thank you.

> *A drumroll.*

> TONY *as* BADGE *bounds forward.*

TONY. I thank you.

> *A drumroll.*

> *Nods to* JOHN.

> I thank you.

> Right?

> *Claps his hands.*

> *Rubs them together eagerly.*

> Training Special Operations Executive Operatives. Secret Agents to you. Somewhere in the Highlands of Scotland.

> Right.

> How to kill an assailant when you are unarmed.

> Form the index and second fingers to a V.

> Approach your assailant.

> Jab him through the eyes. Curl the fingers to hooks, down behind the cheekbones. Squish.

> Bring your foot up upon our assailant's chest.

PUSH with your foot TUG with your fingers. Do this with all your might, pulling off your assailant's facial mask.

He will then be dead.

A drumroll.

I thank you.

Right. After me, with a thrust curl push and pull . . .

TONY *as* BADGE *on an imaginary assailant, quite beside himself. But the three girls,* LINDA, CAROLE *and* AMARYLLIS *standing behind him, deadpan, quietly mime the assault upon themseves — fingers to eyes, pulled down the cheeks, hand on chest.*

And into the song.

Thrust curl push and pull . . . Thrust curl push and pull . . . Thrust curl push and pull . . .

> Thrust curl push and pull
> Remove his natural disguise
> Won't the enemy look a fool
> With the wool of his brains
> Pulled over his eyes

I train them to kill Germans
With everything they find
To gouge and maim and rip off flesh
And leave their front behind

I teach them to enjoy themselves
Believe in what they do
Knowing that the hate they give
Brings peace for me and you

I want to learn to love and kill
Before I kiss my cyanide
To handle butchermeat with ease
And carve my name in flesh and pride

I want to kill a German
I want to do my bit
I want to fight for peace and love
And I am fighting fit

We want to kill a German
We want to do our bit
We want to fight for peace and love
and we are fighting fit

Repeat first chorus.

Phew! Puffed, what?

Right!

Suddenly he lies down.

Got to get a bit crude here ladies. But war is crude! Won on the playing fields of Eton? Bullshit! Backstreets of Glasgow more like.

Points at CAROLE.

You Miss! Stamp on me balls!

CAROLE. Me?

TONY. A − one − two, stamp on me balls a − one − two, come on miss don't be shy. Can't be shy if you're going to kill a man, a − one − two.

CAROLE *comes forward uncertainly.*
Gingerly mimes stamping him in the balls.

Please mean it Miss, mean it.

CAROLE. I'd mean it if you were a Bosch.

TONY. So I'm bloody Himmler, stamp on me balls a − one − two!

She does so, again . . . gingerly.

All right I'm the Bosch that spewed your old man's guts out in the sands a − one − two.

She stamps at BADGE's *balls fiercely at once, expertly he twists, grabs her ankle. They freeze.* BADGE *at once . . .*

That's my lovely girl, that's my lovely good girl.

And they go down in a heap.

TONY *shouts aside to the others:*

Learn from that.

To kill a man, you use YOU and all of YOU − YOU've got.

Your body and your hate.

Crawls towards the other two girls.

The beast, the beast, give the beast reign! Woof woof! Woof woof!

He coughs politely, springs to his feet.

Lightly.

Now let's use our minds.

Turns, toward the audience . . .

When you are in France, you cannot carry a weapon obtrusively. Tommy Gun in the shopping bag, have old Goebbels running all the way from Berlin.

ALL. *Ha ha what a wag the brigadier is.*

TONY. So, no weapons at all. That is, what the army thinks are weapons.

Change, seriously, closer to the audience.

You have to look at the world differently. For you, the hidden enemy in their midst, the whole world is your armoury.

A blow on the drum. The company repeat the slogan.

ALL. THE WHOLE WORLD IS YOUR ARMOURY.

TONY. Look for the sharp, hard edges of everyday objects. Wherever you are, look round and arm yourself.

He taps his head.

In your mind.

Stair rods.

Candle sticks.

And the edge of a saucer can be quite nasty in the teeth.

Violent pulled arm gesture, throwing a discus.

Other ideas!

CAROLE. 'Itting him over the 'ead with a chair.

TONY. Traditional Miss.

AMARYLLIS. Bit corny.

TONY. Don't sneer at it! Ever since the first man sat on the first chair, he's been hitting the second man over the head with it.

CAROLE. Things in the kitchen. Knives, kitchen knives!

TONY. Go on!

CAROLE. Saucepans! Bong on the head.

TONY. Go on!

Go on! Think of them, things to kill a man or maim!

CAROLE. Kettle!

TONY. Go on!

CAROLE. Kettle hot water in his face!

TONY. And!

CAROLE. Cheese grater grater 'cross 'is eyes!

TONY. And!

CAROLE. Potato peeler!

TONY. Potato peeler where!

CAROLE. Anywhere!

TONY. *Potato peeler where!*

CAROLE. Potato peeler . . .

*Hesitates a second. Then coarse, with all the old cruelty
of the playground.*

CAROLE. *In 'is doh dah — in 'is privates — there there there
— cut 'is willy off.*

She points at her crutch, not an imaginary assailant.

A pause.

Then CAROLE *ashamed.*

I'm sorry.

I'm sorry, Sir.

TONY (*gently*): Don't be sorry, my dear. Be glad.

CAROLE. Like . . . Blood in my nails.

From JOHN, *a percussive rasping sound.* CAROLE *claws her
nails in, grates them with her thumb nails.*

The light begins to fade.

TONY *to the audience.*

TONY. One hundred and forty-two gallant men and women
I recruited in the war. One hundred and forty-two gallant
men and women, poked up the German rear.

And of all of them, why she was the tops. The darling.

A real darling — little heroine.

Light going. VIOLETTE's *tension with her fingernails
increasing, also the rasping from* JOHN.

Ladies and gents!

A drum roll.

One more little tip!

Nail file!

He holds one up.

Two centimetres longer than the usual. Issued to all Special
Operatives.

A gesture. On himself.

In the jugular!

One more little tip to stay alive!

The rasping terribly loud.

Light to blackout.

Seventeen

Blackout.

And silence.

KEVIN *as* POTTER *in the blackout* . . .
Only a few seconds. Must get a gun to TONY . . .

TONY *cries out, as* BADGE, *in the dark.*

TONY. OH MOTHER! MOTHER! WHAT'S THAT THING
ON YOUR TIT?

Lights slam up.

BADGE *and* POTTER, *with game rifles.* BADGE *sullen.*

TONY. Bag a bird, Potter.

KEVIN. I don't like to Sir.

TONY. Regimentation of the beast. That's what it's all about.

Realises POTTER'*s spoken. He starts.*

You don't WHAT?

KEVIN. Our family have never liked killing little birds Sir.

TONY. For Godsake.

He's embarrassed.

KEVIN. My father resigned from the local hunt.

TONY. I don't care if he resigned from Heaven. Bag a bird.

KEVIN. No thank you Sir.

TONY. You're about to go too far Potter. You're an intelligent man, but like all intelligent men, you go too far.

KEVIN. Its the principle . . . Of the thing.

BADGE, *aside. In reverie again.*

TONY. Regiments of beastliness. Brigades of pain. When I was eight years old, tootsied up the stair. Been strictly forbidden to, but did.

Took off my little shoes, and tootsied up. To where my mother was . . .

A slight stutter.

P . . . poorly.

Turned the door knob.

Saw one side of her bed, yellow flowers. Other side of her bed, nursie big fat nursie, with great white wads of stuff in her hands, great white wads of stuff. And in her bed.

And in her bed, mother, with her nightie open, and hanging on her chest.

Nursie stepped in front and shouted, and ran at me and pushed me out and slammed the door. But not before I saw mother, with her nightie open and hanging on her chest like a rotten pear. Upside down rotten P . . . P . . . PEAR.

At once out of it.

KEVIN. What if you were a little bird Sir, would you like to be shot at by officers in uniform?

TONY. You're being ridiculous. Bag a bird.

KEVIN. No.

TONY. Balls!

KEVIN. No.

SABIN *at the side as a Sargeant.*

SABIN. Bird up, Suh!

TONY. Go on man!

KEVIN. No!

TONY. For Godsake she's up!

The whish whish of a bird's wings. KEVIN *fires wildly. Two real cartridges.*

A pause.

KEVIN. It . . . Disintegrated.

TONY. What a sportsman calls splattered.

KEVIN. In mid air. Just went apart.

TONY. I'll be honest with you Potter. I don't like you.

KEVIN. I don't like you either Sir.

Lights begin to fade.

TONY. Just got to keep a hold on ourselves. There is a war on.

KEVIN. Sir.

TONY *raises his gun.*

Zooooooooom, Goebbels crotch.

KEVIN. Violette drops tonight.

Looks at his watch. COD OFFICER.

Oh — oh

Indistinct this . . .

Hours.

BADGE *waves the gun.*

TONY. Zooooooooom, Himmler's arsehold.

Lowers the gun.

Plucky girl.

A pause.

Into the dark as it were. Ha.

The lights going fast . . .

And all that.

KEVIN. All that Sir.

TONY. All that.

Eighteen

At once pale, dim blue light on LINDA *as* VIOLETTE.

TONY *changing out of sight into the* HANS *regalia.*

Whispers.

Music. Effects.

AMARYLLIS. Violette.

Pause.

Have you the wireless code for your W/T operator?

The whispers piling up behind . . .

DAVID. Tap tap!

ANGIE. Calling calling!

KEVIN. London London!

SABIN. Deadly peril!

CAROLE. Dead of night!

ANGIE. Hear me dear God hear me!

Pause.

All eyes on LINDA
She nods.

DAVID. I am the Conducting Officer for your section. Please
check your identity and cover, Violette.

Whispers . . .

SABIN. False name!

CAROLE. Fake papers!

SABIN. Lies!

KEVIN. Deceit!

ANGIE. Treachery!

AMARYLLIS. Terror!

LINDA (*matter of fact*): I am Jeanine Culot, from Lyon. I am visiting Rouen to find my cousin.

ANGIE. Are you afraid, Violette?

LINDA. A bit.

Pause.

SABIN. Do you want anything?

LINDA. No.

KEVIN holds his finger and thumb up.

KEVIN. For if they get you.

All look at it.

Get everyone looking.

Old girl.

Death pill, and all that.

AMARYLLIS (*whispers*): Happy Valley Pill . . .

SABIN. No more and no more . . .

CAROLE. Pain!

KEVIN Ter — ror!

LINDA shakes her head.

LINDA. I don't want it.

KEVIN. Brave old thing.

He lowers his hand.

CAROLE. Why are you going?

LINDA. To kill Germans, Ma'am.

CAROLE. Are you afraid?

LINDA. A bit.

KEVIN. Do you want anything?

LINDA. No.

KEVIN. Then . . .

With an old world bow, asking her to leave . . .

Nineteen

Drum.

An aeroplane made by LINDA *as* VIOLETTE, SABIN, CAROLE *and* AMARYLLIS.

Spin out of the aeroplane, into the parachute effect.
All spinning, lit by a beam from floor level, passing through their upraised arms again and again, like a lighthouse beam . . .

Then suddenly LINDA *as the Little Girl.*

LINDA. No!

The beam fixes on her. She breaks from the parachute, crouches as the Little Girl.

Hans Hans . . . Nasty story. You tell me NASTY story.

Why you not tell me NICE story.

She thinks . . .

'Bout . . . 'Bout . . . HEAVEN!

You say you're dead, well the dead go to Heaven don't they. Tell me NICE story 'bout HEAVEN.

Hans!

The beam leaves her, and seeks out TONY *as* HANS, *at the back.*

He points forward.

TONY. Berlin . . .

LINDA. Won't! . . .

TONY. Berlin . . .

LINDA. Won't go horrid Ber-lin. HORRID old man.

TONY *falls on his face.*

TONY. Berlin.

LINDA. Horrid an' nasty. HORRID AN' NASTY, DIRTY OLD MAN.

They'll come an' lock you up. Big police-men, come an' lock you up.

TONY (*reaching forward*). Brandenburger . . .

LINDA. Big police-men come an' say you STOLE me. An' I'll tell 'em you STOLE me and they'll lock you up, dirty old man . . .

HANS. Don't Lin — da . . .

LINDA. Tell me nice story then. 'Bout Heaven.

A pause.

AMARYLLIS (*announcement*). The German soldier tells of a Child's Vision of Heaven.

Lights up.

KEVIN, CAROLE, SABIN *and* AMARYLLIS *sit round* LINDA.

TONY *raises* HANS *to the task. Standing upstage of the circle.*

TONY. Little Linda. Lying asleep at night. And . . .

Pause.

Dream — ing.

Music.

Woke up. Saw by the wardrobe with the big mirror . . .

Pause.

Then quickly.

Saw-by-the-wardrobe-with-the-big-mirror . . . An angel.

LINDA. Was she dead was she dead was she dead . . . ?

TONY. Sort of . . .

A pause.

Dead.

LINDA. But it weren't bad.

TONY. Not bad.

LINDA. It was . . . Lovely! An' what the Angel say, what the Angel say?

AMARYLLIS. The angel said: Climb up on my back.

SABIN. And she did, an' flew out of the window.

LINDA. What, over her back garden?

KEVIN. Over her back garden, and over Mrs Brown's house next door, and over the trees and fields, and up and up.

LINDA. Up the clouds?

AMARYLLIS. Up the clouds.

LINDA. And what's up there then, up the clouds?

SABIN. A big fat man, with a big fat smile . . .

CAROLE. And the big fat man with a big fat smile said . . .

KEVIN. Hello little girl, I'm God.

AMARYLLIS. And so saying, God took out a half pound size paper bag and said . . .

SABIN. Have a sweetie.

CAROLE. And out of the half pound size paper bag God took a *great big gob stopper.*

KEVIN. And Linda looked and looked at the Gob Stopper, and as she looked and looked . . .

AMARYLLIS. God *threw* the gob stopper way up and up . . .

SABIN. Way up and up . . .

CAROLE. Up past the sun and past the moon . . .

KEVIN. And as she looked, the gob stopper turned into a star.

AMARYLLIS. Ah.

ALL. Ah ah . . .

CAROLE. In't that lovely.

KEVIN *blows a raspberry.*

Light begins to change.

TONY, *hands out as* HANS — *Frankenstein, moves towards* LINDA's *back.*

AMARYLLIS. And Linda felt a tickle on her back, and WHOOSH out her little shoulder blades, wings began to sprout, like mushrooms.

LINDA *stands up.*

LINDA. She fly she fly?

AMARYLLIS. Up and up, past the sun and the moon to her
very own star . . .

KEVIN. One billion to the billionth watts of power.

SABIN. Burning . . .

AMARYLLIS. Burning . . .

CAROLE. Burning . . .

KEVIN. Burning . . .

SABIN. Burning . . .

Song
Falling free
the whole world
slips by me
all the things
I've seen and done
have been and gone
and now I'm one
the god of all I see.

Far below
my day is rising
fast although
I'm floating far
across the sky
on magic carpet
questions why
I'll never really know.

Concrete blocks
above my head
grinds my bones
with stones
and rocks
until I'm dead
or wake up
safely home in bed
relieved to know
it's all a dream
and if I scream
an image change
would seem

more welcome
than a naked hallow'en
to a spy
with an X-ray eye
machine

standing still
the sky supports
my wounded will
the angel of
the nylon cloud
I think alone
a blast aloud
of future past
and passing time
to kill

take transfusion
to my mind
try to heal
the wounds of time
or bathe them
in the salt
of many sins
let the entertainment
being.

The song done.

Light change.

Twenty

Blackout.

TONY. Adventure story!

Our scene, occupied France 1944.

Our heroine, Violette.

Dead — of — night. Land in a field.

He switches a hand lamp on her.

LINDA *does a forward roll. Comes out watchful.*

KEVIN.
CAROLE.   Ruuuuuuuuuuuuuuuum, ruuuuuuuum . . .

Motorbike noise coming nearer . . .

TONY. Enemy patrol!

Flick the lamp's beam on KEVIN *and* CAROLE:
KEVIN *as motorbike,* CAROLE *as side car rider . . .*

KEVIN *does the motorbike roar.*

CAROLE. Zieg heil! Zieg heil!

Lamp onto LINDA. *She darts out of the beam. The
'motorbike and side car' skid to a stop in the path of light.
They break out of the motorbike.*

KEVIN. Ja!

Goose step. Extreme parody.

Ein Englander Terrorist landed.

CAROLE. Ja wohl donnerundblitzen zieg heil.

KEVIN. Ludwig Van Beethoven Eine Kleine Nachtmusik!

CAROLE. Zieg!

KEVIN. Ja'.

TONY's *lamp onto* LINDA.

TONY. You hide in a ditch.

All night far and near, you hear the search around the
countryside.

Lamp flicks onto KEVIN *as German soldier dog handler,*
CAROLE *as dog.*

CAROLE. Voof! Voof!

Etc. over KEVIN's . . .

KEVIN. Englander! Ve come to get you, Englander! Ve come
vit dogs!

*Crass parody — but in the torch beam get it as frightening as
possible . . .*

The beam flicks onto LINDA. *She retreats.*

Lamp back on KEVIN *and* CAROLE. *The dog released and
attacks* LINDA.

LINDA *grabs the dog.*

TONY *flicks the lamp up into his own face — he's excited.*

TONY. Back legs, pull em! Kill a dog, every soldier every slum kid in Europe knows that. To kill a dog pull the back legs apart! Snap the spine!

Lamp onto LINDA *and* CAROLE *again.*

CAROLE *dead still.*

LINDA *backing away from the dog.*

And TONY *gently narrates.*

And Violette, dragged the dead dog to a thicket, so it wouldn't be found. And all night, in the rain, kept silent. She got away then.

Sadly.

But we got her in the end. Ja ja.

Lights slam up.

Twenty-One

Lights up. Bright and hard — all over.

The two scenes, 'Keiffer's Interrogation' and 'The Adventure in the Field', are played with one scene frozen into the other.

SABIN. Violette's interrogation. Gestapo Headquarters, Avenue Foch, Paris.

S.S. Sturnbann Führer Hans Josef Keiffer.

He turns to her. She stares back.

A pause.

Then AMARYLLIS *turns aside.*

AMARYLLIS. They put a thing in Violette's mouth.

AMARYLLIS *jerks. Mouth clammed.*

At once SABIN *comes round to face her. Concerned.*

SABIN. Don't bite on it, or you'll choke OK? Just don't bite. Nod if you get that.

She tears at the gag shaking her head vehemently.

Don't Vi don't Vi, we'll only tie it in.

She stops and stares at him.
Arms sharply down, fists clenched.

Or.

A light gesture.

A strap. Handcuffs. Some . . .

With a sigh.

Kind of harness.

Light and reasonable.

Just want to hear the sound of my own voice for a little,
alright Vi? Right? Alright?

Vi?

Pause, as he circles: and suddenly, speaking fast, elaborately.

You are an English girl with a French mother. Agent,
dropped in France, the succour and aid the enemies of the
Reich. The Salon-La-Tour area? Yes? Yes.

What fields have been selected for further landings?

When you left England, what instructions were you carrying?

And what is the code used by your radio operator? For every
wireless operator has his code, so what is his code?

There is also the question of the expected landings in the
South of France. Ten Panzer Divisions have been in the
South. Have the landings been abandoned, or are they to be
made, now that these Divisions have been moved to the
North? It is a vital question, and we are convinced that
an agent strategically placed between North and South must
be able to supply the answer, etcetera.

Etcetera etcetera his words
pour out over the gagged girl.

Silence.

SABIN *looks up at her. Slowly he yawns, then* KEIFFER's
talking again, quieter this time, and lower.

There is only one end, Vi, to these scenes between us.
Confession, and the mutilation of your sweet self.

Blindness, spinal deformity, nose cut open, teeth all out, feet cut off, hands too. All things come to pass, one . . .

Gesture, as if to an outsider.

summer afternoon in Paris.

And he shrugs.

But . . . Let's be . . .

With a curious, precise movement — like changing a car gear.

Realistic.

At once strides to her. Takes the gag out — close to her now, but not looking at her, as if walking past her.

AMARYLLIS. Instructions to Captured Operatives — Resist — Remember, there is no blame.

As VIOLETTE *at once, spits on* KEIFFER's *cheek.*

Hang you. When England's won the war they'll hang you. An English judge, he'll put a black cap on his head. That's what they do when they condemn a foul evil murderer like you to death.

SABIN. Simple as that.

VIOLETTE. You bet.

She spits this out at him . . . fast.

An' I know about the pliars. Going to tear out my nails.

Sarcasm.

'Fore you cut off my hands o' course, and you have special pliars don't you. Gestapo gets 'em from a factory near Dresden. WELL the R.A.F. knows where the factory is, and they're going to bomb it.

SABIN *hits her with a great sweeping gesture.* AMARYLLIS's VIOLETTE *falls away.*

SABIN (*with a dead voice*). Silly — little — girl. Its all . . . Propaganda and defeat.

Blackout.

Twenty-Two

In the dark — only the lamp.

TONY. Anastasie!

Lamp on KEVIN.

CAROLE. Your name is Jacques Dufour. Maquis leader. Code name Anastasie.

TONY. Violette!

CAROLE. Rendezvous.

Music.

KEVIN *and* LINDA *dance.*

TONY *calls out, like a square dance caller.* CAROLE *lays the actions on them.*

TONY. True story! Gun battle and capture!

CAROLE. Driving alone a country lane!

TONY. Sunlight glints on a German helmet, a hundred yards ahead!

CAROLE. Stop the car! Get out! Keep your heads down! Into the hedge!

TONY. Ambush, raus raus!

CAROLE. Run across the field!

TONY. Here they come, HUNDREDS of 'em!

CAROLE. Vi, you fell! Ankle gone!

TONY. And open fire!

CAROLE. Coming up the hill, they're coming up the hill, like a hoard of rats!

TONY. Say goodbye!

CAROLE. Vi you say go on without me! Anastasie you say no! Go for all we love!

TONY. Kiss me!

CAROLE. Goodbye my love, and he runs to safety!

TONY. Gunbattle!

CAROLE. Vi you lie in the grass, in the field, turn with your gun and kill and kill and kill and . . .

Sudden dead stop to the music.

TONY *now close to* LINDA.

Very deliberately, quietly.

TONY. Dead German soldiers lying in the field.
No more bullets in her gun.
Caught.
Animal . . . in . . . trap.

He opens his arms to her. They freeze.

Lights up.

TONY, LINDA, CAROLE, KEVIN *hold still while the*
VI − KEIFFER *pieces are played. The two fold together.*

TONY *is in position at the end of this scene ready for the
last scene.*

Twenty-Three

Lights up.

A brief passage of cross-talk.

Deadpan.

SABIN. You fell, twisted your ankle.	AMARYLLIS.
Gave Anastasie covering fire.	
Please repeat that.	I don't see the point.
All I want is a fact, a simple fact. May I smoke?	There's no point in that.

Pause.

	You will if you want to.
All I want to do, Vi. Is get at the reality of the situation. What?	Are you frightened of something?

You heard.

Vi, tell me simply, what
do you believe in?
I mean are there any   None of your business.
thoughts you may have?   None of your business!

Doubts?
It's a rather amusing   They'll hang you, pervert!
situation.   pervert!
I'm rather excited by it.
A stereotyped situation,
like a dance, I trained as
a dancer.   Vile!
Always been musical.

*He clicks his finger in
his ear.*

G Flat. Perfect pitch you
see.   Vile pervert!

And SABIN *breaks away,* KEIFFER *angry.*

A pause.

He turns on her. With all his insidious urbanity.

SABIN. Oh Vi.

With a bow.

Nazi Gestapo Torturer. Victim. After the War, torturer and
victim will be seen as something sexy.

VIOLETTE, *vehemently.*

AMARYLLIS. That's just nasty.

SABIN. There'll be a trade. Like antiques. Nazi thumbscrews,
collectors' pieces.

AMARYLLIS. You're sick, just sick.

SABIN. You and I, Vi, will give people a sexy thrill.

Is he going to tear her nipples out with red hot tongs now,
or later?

AMARYLLIS. You're sick. You . . .

She searches for the word.

Defile things.

SABIN. Silly bitch.

Fast, close to her.

Oh Vi, there's no 'magnificent gesture' that can't be defiled. Mucked. Messed. Believe me, Miss Heroine, all pure. The hero, hung over the fires, in the cellar of the Avenue Foch, blind and silent.

AMARYLLIS. SICK. SICK.

SABIN. So simple for Violette.

Sarcastically.

Saint Joan! Banners! The people's heroic darling! And for me, Me Villain, leering over the rack . . .

Dismissive.

Perhaps in the 1960's I'll be arrested in Buenos Aires. Grey, fat, ugly. The newspaper photographs will reflect 'steely blue eyes.'

Change.

Please hear why the Gestapo never tortured you, in the Avenue Foch. Why that scene in the film, never took place.

Because . . . Of administrative confusion. They lost your papers, Violette. That is why you were never sent for again, by Hans Josef Keiffer.

A small bow.

Blackout.

Twenty-Four

Blackout.

TONY. Linda — Linda. River Rhine.

LINDA. I wanna go home.

TONY. River Rhine.

LINDA. Wanna go home.

TONY. Rhine!

LINDA. S'only a ditch silly old man.

TONY *on his knees, by* LINDA.

Silly silly old man, silly silly rotting old dirty old DEAD MAN.

HANS *points.*

TONY. Huh!

LINDA. What now?

TONY. Far Bank! Fatherland!

Calls from the rest of the company.
Whistles. Dogbarks.

ALL. Linda! Linda! Where are you?!

A single beam from the back. Sweeps over TONY *and* LINDA. TONY *his hands round the little girl's neck.*

The beam passes then TONY *standing.*

The din of dogs whistles and calls.

With LINDA *limp in his arms,* TONY *shouts over the din.*

TONY. Führer my Führer, I hear you my Führer, dancing on my grave.

Music. Rises to a crescendo.

Silence.

AMARYLLIS. Violette Szabo was executed at Ravensbruck Concentration Camp on the 25th of January, 1945.

A pause.

Hitler dances.

Music continues.

The company take off any masks etc. and leave them on the stage.

The band play 'The Hitler Dances Song.'

Can you hear
The voices calling
Can you see
The buildings falling
Rising from the ruins
The carrion cabal
Dancing on the banks
Of the boiling canal

You seek the king
But find the knave
If you're searching
For an answer
Watch the phantom dancer
Dancing on your grave

Generations lying
While Europe's dying
Day is drawing near
The figureheads are frowning
While all the world
Is drowning in a tear
The wisdom of the sages
Has prophesised
The century of fear
Here come dark ages
The children of the antichrist
Are here

Strands of morse
From a sattelite
The dawn is gone
Approach the night
Burning telegrams
From the moon
The germs are dining
Feet and soon
You seek the king
But find the knave
If you're searching
For the answer
Ask the phantom dancer
Dancing on your grave.

The song ends with the tat the company used lying about the stage.

No curtain call.

End.

Methuen's Modern Plays

Jean Anouilh	*Antigone*
	Becket
	The Lark
John Arden	*Serjeant Musgrave's Dance*
	The Workhouse Donkey
	Armstrong's Last Goodnight
John Arden and	*The Business of Good Government*
Margaretta D'Arcy	*The Royal Pardon*
	The Hero Rises Up
	The Island of the Mighty
	Vandaleur's Folly
Wolfgang Bauer	*Shakespeare the Sadist*
Rainer Werner	
Fassbinder	*Bremen Coffee,*
Peter Handke	*My Foot My Tutor,*
Frank Xaver Kroetz	*Stallerhof*
Brendan Behan	*The Quare Fellow*
	The Hostage
	Richard's Cork Leg
Edward Bond	*A-A-America!* and *Stone*
	Saved
	Narrow Road to the Deep North
	The Pope's Wedding
	Lear
	The Sea
	Bingo
	The Fool and *We Come to the River*
	Theatre Poems and Songs
	The Bundle
	The Woman
	The Worlds with *The Activists Papers*
	Restoration and *The Cat*
	Summer
Bertolt Brecht	*Mother Courage and Her Children*
	The Caucasian Chalk Circle
	The Good Person of Szechwan
	The Life of Galileo
	The Threepenny Opera
	Saint Joan of the Stockyards
	The Resistible Rise of Arturo Ui
	The Mother

	The Ride Across Lake Constance
	They Are Dying Out
Barrie Keeffe	*Gimme Shelter (Gem, Gotcha, Getaway)*
	Barbarians (Killing Time, Abide With Me, In the City)
	A Mad World, My Masters
Arthur Kopit	*Indians*
	Wings
John McGrath	*The Cheviot, the Stag and the Black, Black Oil*
David Mercer	*After Haggerty*
	The Bankrupt and other plays
	Cousin Vladimir and *Shooting the Chandelier*
	Duck Song
	The Monster of Karlovy Vary and *Then and Now*
	No Limits To Love
Peter Nichols	*Passion Play*
	Poppy
Joe Orton	*Loot*
	What the Butler Saw
	Funeral Games and *The Good and Faithful Servant*
	Entertaining Mr Sloane
	Up Against It
Harold Pinter	*The Birthday Party*
	The Room and *The Dumb Waiter*
	The Caretaker
	A Slight Ache and other plays
	The Collection and *The Lover*
	The Homecoming
	Tea Party and other plays
	Landscape and *Silence*
	Old Times
	No Man's Land
	Betrayal
	The Hothouse
Luigi Pirandello	*Henry IV*
	Six Characters in Search of an Author
Stephen Poliakoff	*Hitting Town* and *City Sugar*
David Rudkin	*The Sons of Light*
	The Triumph of Death

Jean-Paul Sartre	*Crime Passionnel*
Wole Soyinka	*Madmen and Specialists*
	The Jero Plays
	Death and the King's Horseman
C.P. Taylor	*And a Nightingale Sang . . .*
	Good
Nigel Williams	*Line 'Em*
	Class Enemy
Charles Wood	*Veterans*
Theatre Workshop	*Oh What a Lovely War!*
Various authors	*Best Radio Plays of 1978* (Don Haworth: *Episode on a Thursday Evening:* Tom Mallin: *Halt! Who Goes There?;* Jennifer Phillips: *Daughters of Men;* Fay Weldon: *Polaris;* Jill Hyem: *Remember Me;* Richard Harris: *Is It Something I Said?)*
	Best Radio Plays of 1979 (Shirley Gee: *Typhoid Mary;* Carey Harrison: *I Never Killed My German;* Barrie Keeffe: *Heaven Scent;* John Kirkmorris: *Coxcomb;* John Peacock: *Attard in Retirement;* Olwen Wymark: *The Child)*
	Best Radio Plays of 1980 (Stewart Parker: *The Kamikaze Ground Staff Reunion Dinner;* Martyn Read: *Waving to a Train;* Peter Redgrave: *Martyr of the Hives;* William Trevor: *Beyond the Pale)*

The Master Playwrights

Collections of plays by the best-known modern playwrights in value-for-money paperbacks.

| John Arden | PLAYS: ONE |
| | *Serjeant Musgrave's Dance, The Workhouse Donkey, Armstrong's Last Goodnight* |

Harold Pinter	PLAYS: ONE
	The Birthday Party, The Room, The Dumb
	Waiter, A Slight Ache, A Night Out
	PLAYS: TWO
	The Caretaker, Night School, The Dwarfs,
	The Collection, The Lover, five revue sketches
	PLAYS: THREE
	The Homecoming, Tea Party, The Basement,
	Landscape, Silence, six revue sketches
	PLAYS: FOUR
	Old Times, No Man's Land, Betrayal,
	Monologue, Family Voices
Terence Rattigan	PLAYS: ONE
	French Without Tears, The Winslow Boy,
	The Browning Version, Harlequinade
Strindberg	*Introduced and translated by Michael Meyer*
	THE FATHER, MISS JULIE, THE GHOST
	SONATA
	PLAYS TWO
	The Dance of Death, A Dream Play, The
	Stronger
J.M. Synge	THE COMPLETE PLAYS
	In the Shadow of the Glen, Riders to the
	Sea, The Tinker's Wedding, The Well of the
	Saints, The Playboy of the Western World,
	Deirdre of the Sorrows
Oscar Wilde	THREE PLAYS
	Lady Windermere's Fan, An Ideal Husband,
	The Importance of Being Earnest

*If you would like to receive, free of charge, regular information
about new plays and theatre books from Methuen, please send
your name and address to:*

The Marketing Department (Drama)
Methuen London Ltd
North Way
Andover
Hampshire SP10 5BE